Table of Contents

Benchmark Papers and Instructional Support

Using This Book

Part A: Support for Open-Response Questions

STRATEGIES FOR ANSWERING OPEN-RESPONSE QUESTIONS

This section includes three five-page lessons designed to prepare children to answer different types of open-response questions that may appear on reading tests. These lessons practice three skills that are commonly assessed with either short-response or long-response questions. The lessons can be used in any order.

Skill
Identifying main idea and supporting details
Using words and pictures
Understanding stories

Lesson Organization Each lesson includes two blackline masters and three pages of teaching support. Copy and distribute page A2 for children to use with all lessons.

• **Student Lesson Pages** The first blackline master provides a reading passage followed by two open-response questions. Question 1 requires a short-response answer of one or two sentences. Question 2 requires a longer response of several sentences. To model strong and weak responses, a second blackline master for each lesson provides two sample answers to the long-response question. A scoring analysis for each sample response provides details that you can use to discuss with children why each answer deserved its rating.

• **Teaching Support** The teaching support pages offer suggestions for guiding children through a four-step process to respond to each open-response question. These four steps are also provided on a blackline master, page A2.

Annotations The blue annotations that appear on each reading passage highlight the details that relate to questions 1 and 2 on that page. **These annotations should not reproduce on a light or a normal setting but most likely will show on dark settings.**

• Make these pages into overhead transparencies with or without the annotations and use them to guide discussion.

• Duplicate the pages on a normal or a light setting. Have children mark their own copies.

PRACTICE TESTS

Three practice tests are included in blackline master format. These practice tests provide practice with both short- and long-response questions. The answer key identifies which skill each item addresses.

Part B: Support for Writing Tests

READING THE PROMPT

This section is designed to help children analyze and determine appropriate responses to the types of prompts—descriptive, narrative, expository, and persuasive—that may be assessed on writing tests. (Narrative writing has been separated into **personal narrative** and **story.** In addition, the type of expository writing referred to in this book as an **opinion essay** is sometimes called an **explanation** or a **personal essay.**) A pair of instructional pages is provided for each type of writing. These pairs of pages for each writing type can be used in any order.

A final group of pages provides instruction and practice with prompts representing the different types of writing.

ELABORATION STRATEGIES PRACTICE

These pages provide practice with proven strategies that will help children raise their scores on writing tests.

BENCHMARK PAPERS, RUBRICS, AND SCORING ANALYSES

Benchmark Papers The benchmark papers represent scores of 4, 3, 2, 1, and Unscorable for each type of writing. (Errors in conventions have been corrected to help children concentrate on focus, organization, support or elaboration, and sentence variety.)

Consider these options for using the benchmark papers with children.
- Make the paper into an overhead transparency to use for discussion.
- Duplicate individual copies for children to mark as you discuss the paper with them. Help them locate and highlight strengths: a sense of completeness and wholeness, clear organizational pattern, freshness of expression, mature language, effective elaboration, varied sentence structure, transitional words, interesting dialogue, and particularly strong openings and closings.

Scoring Rubrics A four-point rubric specific to the type of writing follows each set of benchmark papers.

Analyses An analysis of the score is provided for each paper and can be used to guide children in recognizing the paper's strengths and weaknesses. Cross-references to *Houghton Mifflin Reading* and *Houghton Mifflin English* components for more instructional support use these codes: **PE** (pupil edition), **TE** (*Teacher's Edition*), **PB** (*Practice Book*), **WP** (*Workbook Plus*), **RW** (*Reteaching Workbook*), and **SWT** (this book).

Preparing for Writing Tests: *Houghton Mifflin Reading*

Houghton Mifflin Reading		Support for Writing Tests
Theme	Test-Related Instruction	Related Support
Theme 1: Silly Stories *4–6 weeks for entire theme*	**Selection 1:** *Dragon Gets By* Story Structure, TE *2.1* pp. 17, 33, 41A–41B	• Answering Open-Response Questions, p. A2 • Open-Response Questions: Understanding Stories, pp. A13–A17
	Reading-Writing Workshop: Story, TE *2.1* pp. 42–43G	• Benchmark Papers: Story, pp. B38–B45 • Reading a Story Prompt, pp. B4–B5 • Elaboration Strategies, pp. B22, B26
	Taking Tests: Choosing the Best Answer, PE *2.1* pp. 112–113	
Theme 2: Nature Walk *4–6 weeks for entire theme*	**Selection 1:** *Henry and Mudge and the Starry Night* Using a Map, TE *2.1* pp. 153E–153F	• Open-Response Questions: Words and Pictures, pp. A8–A12
	Reading-Writing Workshop: Description, TE *2.1* pp. 154–155G	• Benchmark Papers: Description, pp. B53–B59 • Reading a Description Prompt, pp. B8–B9 • Elaboration Strategies, pp. B21, B27, B28
	Taking Tests: Filling in the Blank, PE *2.1* pp. 210–211	• Practice Test, pp. A18–A19
Theme 3: Around Town: Neighborhood and Community *4–6 weeks for entire theme*	**Selection 2:** *A Trip to the Firehouse* Topic, Main Idea, and Supporting Details, TE *2.1* pp. 267, 281, 295A–295B	• Open-Response Questions: Main Idea and Supporting Details, pp. A3–A7
	Writing Skills: Writing to Persuade, TE *2.1* pp. 367M–367N	• Benchmark Papers: Persuasive Essay, pp. B67–B73 • Reading a Persuasive Prompt, pp. B12–B13 • Elaboration Strategies, p. B30
	Taking Tests: Writing a Personal Response, PE *2.1* pp. 368–369	
Theme 4: Amazing Animals *4–6 weeks for entire theme*	**Taking Tests: Vocabulary,** PE *2.2* pp. 116–117	• Practice Test, pp. A20–A21
Theme 5: Family Time *4–6 weeks for entire theme*	**Writing Skills: An Opinion Paragraph,** TE *2.2* pp. 151M–151N	
	Reading-Writing Workshop: Personal Narrative, TE *2.2* pp. 152–153G	• Benchmark Papers: Personal Narrative, pp. B31–B37 • Reading a Personal Narrative Prompt, pp. B2–B3 • Elaboration Strategies, pp. B19, B20
	Taking Tests: Writing an Answer, PE *2.2* pp. 262–263	

Theme 6: Talent Show 4–6 weeks for entire theme	Writing Skills: A Paragraph That Explains, TE *2.2* pp. 325M–325N	• Benchmark Papers: Opinion Essay/ Explanation, pp. B69–B77 • Reading an Opinion/Explanation Prompt, pp. B10–B11 • Elaboration Strategies, pp. B23, B29
	Reading-Writing Workshop: Instructions, TE *2.2* pp. 326–327G	• Benchmark Papers: Instructions, pp. B46–B52 • Reading an Instructions Prompt, pp. B6–B7 • Elaboration Strategies, pp. B24, B25 • Reading Prompts, pp. B14–B15 • Writing Prompts, pp. B16–B18
	Taking Tests: Writing a Personal Narrative, PE *2.2* pp. 398–399	• Practice Test, pp. A22–A23

Preparing for Writing Tests: *Houghton Mifflin English*

Houghton Mifflin English	Support for Writing Tests	
Writing Unit	Open-Response Questions	Writing to a Prompt
Unit 2: Writing a Personal Narrative 2 weeks for pp. 63–81	• Answering Open-Response Questions, p. A2 • Open-Response Questions: Main Idea and Supporting Details, pp. A3–A7 • Practice Test, pp. A18–A19	• Benchmark Papers: Personal Narrative, pp. B31–B37 • Reading a Personal Narrative Prompt, pp. B2–B3 • Elaboration Strategies, pp. B19, B20
Unit 4: Writing a Story 2 weeks for pp. 135–155	• Open-Response Questions: Understanding Stories, pp. A13–A17 • Practice Test, pp. A20–A21	• Benchmark Papers: Story, pp. B38–B45 • Reading a Story Prompt, pp. B4–B5 • Elaboration Strategies, pp. B22, B26
Unit 6: Writing Instructions 2 weeks for pp. 207–223	• Open-Response Questions: Words and Pictures, pp. A8–A12 • Practice Test, pp. A22–A23	• Benchmark Papers: Instructions, pp. B46–B52 • Reading an Instructions Prompt, pp. B6–B7 • Elaboration Strategies, pp. B24, B25
Unit 8: Writing a Description 2 weeks for pp. 267–285		• Benchmark Papers: Description, pp. B53–B59 • Reading a Description Prompt, pp. B8–B9 • Elaboration Strategies, pp. B21, B27, B28
Unit 10: Writing to Express an Opinion 2 weeks for pp. 341–359		• Benchmark Papers: Opinion Essay/ Explanation, pp. B60–B66 • Reading an Opinion/Explanation Prompt, pp. B10–B11 • Elaboration Strategies, pp. B23, B29
(Unit 10) Special Focus on Influencing: Writing to Persuade 1 week for pp. 362–369		• Benchmark Papers: Persuasive Essay, pp. B67–B73 • Reading a Persuasive Prompt, pp. B12–B13 • Elaboration Strategies, p. B30

Note The writing units in Houghton Mifflin English *can be used in any order. The lessons focusing on answering Open-Response Questions are self-contained and can be taught at any time and in any order.*

PART
A

Support for
Open-Response Questions

Strategies for Answering
Open-Response Questions

Practice Tests

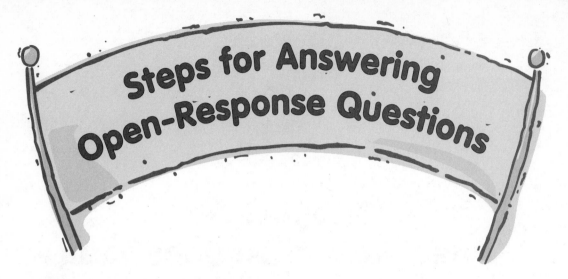

Steps for Answering Open-Response Questions

1 **READ THE QUESTION.**

Look for clues that tell what to write about.

2 **SEARCH AND FIND.**

Look for details that answer the question.

3 **GET READY TO WRITE.**

Make notes. List details from the story that answer the question.

4 **WRITE YOUR ANSWER.**

✔ Use the clue words from the question.

✔ Use details and words from the story.

✔ Write only what you need to answer the question.

Test Tip
Don't worry! If a question seems hard, just follow these steps.

Main Idea and Supporting Details

Explain that the **main idea** tells what a story is mostly about. **Supporting details** tell more about the main idea.

Reading the Question

Tell children that test questions include clue words that will tell them what to do. Some examples are shown in the chart. Explain that *who, where,* and *when* usually ask for supporting details. Other clue words will tell them what they should write about.

Clue Words for Main Idea and Supporting Details
main idea, title, mostly about, what, who, where, when, why, which, how

The sample questions below are the kind that might appear with a passage on a test. Put the chart and the questions on the board. Then use the Think Aloud to model how to analyze the questions.

- What is the main idea of the story "Melissa's Messy Room"?
- When did Kevin learn that the dog could talk?

Think Aloud
- I see in the first question the clue words *main idea,* so this question is asking me about the most important idea. Now I look for clue words that tell me what to write about. I see the words *the story "Melissa's Messy Room."* To answer this question, I will write what the story "Melissa's Messy Room" is mainly about.
- I see the clue word *When* in the second question, so it is probably about supporting details. The clue words *Kevin learn that the dog could talk* tell me what to write about. I will write about when Kevin learned that the dog could talk.

Answering the Question

Question 1 Duplicate pages A2, A6, and A7. Distribute pages A2 and A6. Have children read the story "The Lion Pride." (You might want children to number the paragraphs.) Explain that page A2 shows the four steps children should use to answer the questions. Work with children to answer question 1, a short-answer question, using the steps.

Steps for Answering Open-Response Questions

1 READ THE QUESTION

Have children find the clue words in the question. Use the prompts below.
- Circle the clue words that tell whether the question is asking about the main idea and about supporting details. *[main idea]*
- Circle the clue words that tell what to write about. *[the story "The Lion Pride"]*
- What does this question ask you to write about? [the main idea of the story "The Lion Pride"]

more ➡

Main Idea and Supporting Details *(continued)*

2 SEARCH AND FIND

Tell children that in many stories the main idea is only hinted at. Readers have to read carefully to figure out the main idea. Explain that hints or clues about the main idea are often found at the beginning or at the end of the story. Sometimes these hints or clues are found in both places. Tell children to look in both places for words or sentences that best tell the main idea of the story. Use the prompt below.

• Which sentence helps you know what the story is mainly about? Underline this sentence. **[Children should underline the last sentence in paragraph 1.]**

3 GET READY TO WRITE

Work with children to make notes, listing key points from the story. On the board, model making a list of key points that answer the question.

[Main idea of story "The Lion Pride"
– Lions are the only cats that live in families.]

4 WRITE YOUR ANSWER

Review the guidelines under Step 4 on page A2. Tell children to follow them when writing their answers. Show children how to use their list of key points to write a clear and complete response to question 1. Write the sample answer on the board. **[*Sample high-scoring response*: The main idea of the story "The Lion Pride" is that lions are the only cats that live in families.]** Ask children to compare the answer to each point in the guidelines.

Question 2 Work with children to use Steps 1–3 to answer question 2 on page A6. Explain that this is a long-answer question, which requires children to write more. When you reach Step 4, distribute page A7, which shows sample answers for question 2. Answers to Steps 1–4 are given below.

1 READ THE QUESTION

[Children should circle *Who* (clue word for supporting details) and *belongs to a lion pride* (clue words for what to write about). The question asks who belongs to the lion pride.]

2 SEARCH AND FIND

[Children should underline sentences 2, 3, and 4 in paragraph 2.]

more ➡

Main Idea and Supporting Details *(continued)*

❸ GET READY TO WRITE

[Who belongs to a lion pride
– father lion
– mother lion, or lioness
– babies, or cubs]

❹ WRITE YOUR ANSWER

[Children should circle paragraph B.] These scoring analyses explain the score of each sample answer.

Sample Answer A This response indicates that the student has a very limited understanding of the question. The student explains that a lion family can have two, three, or four cubs. However, the student never mentions that a mother and father lion are also part of a lion family.

Sample Answer B This top-scoring response provides a complete, accurate description of who belongs to a lion pride (*a father lion, a mother lion, and babies*). The student includes details about what a mother lion is called (*lioness*) and what the babies are called (*cubs*).

Try It Out

Children can use the Practice Tests on pages A18–A23 for more practice answering open-response questions.

Name _____

Main Idea and Supporting Details

The Lion Pride

1   There are little cats, and there are big cats. Little cats meow. Big cats roar. Lions are big cats that live in Africa. They like to be together. Lions are the only cats that live in families.

2   A lion family is called a pride. A pride can have a father lion, a mother lion, and babies. The mother lion is called a lioness. Baby lions are called cubs. A mother lion can have two or three cubs. Sometimes she has four. Some cubs stay in the pride all their lives. Other cubs leave the pride when they are almost grown.

3   The mother lion does most of the hunting. Lions eat large animals such as deer and zebras. They also eat fish and birds. When it's time to eat, the father lion eats first. Then the mother lion eats. Last of all, the cubs eat.

4   The father lion guards the family. He has long shaggy hair around his neck. This is called a mane. This makes him look big and dangerous. He also has a loud roar. This makes other animals afraid. That is why he is called the King of Animals.

5   Lions sleep most of the day. The pride stays close together. Cubs play and tumble with each other. They chase their mother's tail. Lions seem to like living in their large family.

Q 1

Q 2

Answer these questions about the story above.

SHORT RESPONSE   **1.** What is the main idea of the story "The Lion Pride"? Use details from the story in your answer.

LONG RESPONSE   **2.** Who belongs to a lion pride? Use details from the story in your answer.

See page i for notes about the annotations and ideas for using the page.

Name _____

Main Idea and Supporting Details

 Read these answers to question 2 on page A6. Circle the answer that tells all the members of a lion pride.

A A lion family can have two or three cubs. Sometimes there are four cubs. The cubs play with each other.

B A lion pride can have a father lion, a mother lion, and babies. The mother lion is called a lioness. The babies are called cubs.

Words and Pictures

Explain that photographs, illustrations, and other kinds of pictures, such as maps, charts, graphs, and diagrams, can be used to add information to written materials.

Reading the Question

Tell children that test questions include clue words that will tell them what to do. Some examples are shown in the chart. Other clue words will tell them what they should write about. The sample question below is the kind that might appear with a passage on a test. Put the chart and the question on the board. Then use the Think Aloud to model how to analyze the question.

Clue Words for Using Pictures
look at, picture, drawing, map, chart

• How do you make a banana split? Use details from the story and the picture in your answer.

Think Aloud

• In this question, I see the words *details from the story and the picture*, so this question is asking me to use the words and the picture to find details. When I look for clue words that tell me what to write about, I see the words *make a banana split*. I will write about how to make a banana split, using the story and the picture to help me.

Answering the Question

Question 1 Duplicate pages A2, A11, and A12 and distribute pages A2 and A11. Have children read "Mike Finds Help." (You might want children to number the paragraphs.) Explain that page A2 shows the four steps children should use to answer the questions. Work with children to answer question 1, a short-answer question, using the steps.

Steps for Answering Open-Response Questions

1 READ THE QUESTION

Have children find the clue words in the question. Use the prompts below.
• Circle the clue words that tell you to use both words and pictures. *[details from the story and the picture]*
• Circle clue words that tell what to write about. *[How does the robot move]*
• What does this question ask you to write about? **[what the story and the picture tell about how the robot moves]**

---

more ➡

Words and Pictures *(continued)*

❷ SEARCH AND FIND

Point out that pictures may include information that is not found in the story and that the story often includes information that is not in the pictures. Help children review the picture and the story for details. Use the prompts below.

- Which details in the story will help you explain how the robot moves? Underline these details. **[Children should underline the last sentence in paragraph 4.]**
- Circle the part of the picture that will help you explain how the robot moves. **[Children should circle the robot's wheels.]**

❸ GET READY TO WRITE

Work with children to make notes, listing details from the picture and the story. On the board, model making a list of details that answer the question.

[How robot moves
– forward and backward
– on wheels]

❹ WRITE YOUR ANSWER

Review the guidelines under Step 4 of page A2. Tell children to follow them when writing their answers. Show children how to use their list to write a clear and complete response to question 1. Write the sample answer on the board. **[*Sample high-scoring response*: The robot can move forward and backward. It moves on wheels.]** Ask children to compare the answer to each point in the guidelines.

Question 2 Work with children to use Steps 1–3 to answer question 2 on page A11. Explain that this is a long-answer question, which requires children to write more. When you reach Step 4, distribute page A12, which shows sample answers for question 2. Answers for Steps 1–4 are given below.

❶ READ THE QUESTION

[Children should circle *details from the story and the picture* (clue words for using words and pictures) and *How is the robot like a person* (clue words for what to write about). Help them understand that they will need to use information from both the story and the picture to write about how a robot and a person are alike.]

❷ SEARCH AND FIND

[Children should underline the last sentence in paragraph 4 again. They should also underline paragraph 5. They should circle the face and arms in the picture.]

more ➡

Words and Pictures (continued)

 GET READY TO WRITE

[How robot and person are alike
What they do
– move forward and backward
– pick up things
– put things away
– make a bed
How they look
– have face
– have arms]

④ WRITE YOUR ANSWER

[Children should circle paragraph A.] These scoring analyses explain the score of each sample answer.

Sample Answer A This top-scoring response provides a complete, accurate description of how the robot is like a person. The student uses details from the passage to describe how the robot acts like a person (*can move forward and backward; pick up things; put things away; make a bed*). The student uses details from the passage to describe how the robot looks like a person. (*They each have a face and arms.*)

Sample Answer B This response includes general statements about how the robot in the passage is like a person (*can do a lot of the same things; robot looks like a person*). However, the student offers no details from the passage about what the robot can do and offers no details from the picture about how the robot resembles a person.

Try It Out

Students can use the Practice Tests on pages A18–A23 for more practice answering open-response questions.

Name _____

Words and Pictures

Mike Finds Help

1   Mike didn't like Saturdays. On Saturdays he had to clean his room. His room wasn't really dirty. There was just a lot of stuff everywhere!

2   Mike always forgot to hang up his clothes. He left books and toys all over the floor, and he never made his bed. Putting everything away made Mike want to cry. Mike needed help!

3   One day Mike saw an ad in a magazine. The ad was for a robot that can clean a messy room. "What a great idea!" thought Mike. "I want one of those."

4   Mike read more about the robot. It is made of heavy plastic and has shiny buttons and bright lights. It will do whatever a person tells it to do. The robot can move forward and backward.

5   The robot can do different jobs. It can pick up things and put them away. It can even make a bed.

6   "The robot is almost like a real person," thought Mike. "It can do just about anything. In some ways, it even looks like a person."

7   Mike ran to find his mother. "I know what I want for my birthday," he said. He showed her the ad. "Please get it for me. I'll even let YOU use it sometimes."

Answer these questions about the story above.

SHORT RESPONSE **1.** How does the robot move? Use details from the story and the picture in your answer.

LONG RESPONSE **2.** How is the robot like a person? Use details from the story and the picture in your answer.

See page i for notes about the annotations and ideas for using the page.

Name _____

Words and Pictures

 LONG RESPONSE Read these answers to question 2 on page A11. Circle the answer that tells how the robot is like a person and that gives details about how the two are alike.

A This is how the robot is like a person. Both the robot and a person can move forward and backward, can pick up things, can put things away, and can make a bed. The robot sort of looks like a person too. They each have a face and arms.

B Both the robot and a person can do a lot of the same things. They can both move around. The robot looks like a person in some ways too.

Understanding Stories

Remind children that characters are the people, animals, or creatures in a story. Events are what the characters do or what happens to them.

Reading the Question

Tell children that test questions might ask them to write about characters or events in a story. Clue words will tell them what they are to write about. The sample questions below are the kind that might appear with a passage on a test. Put the questions on the board. Then use the Think Aloud to model how to analyze them.

- Why did Luís want the biggest part in the school play?
- What happened during Jennifer's music lesson?

Think Aloud

- I see that the first question asks about a person, or character, in the story. A clue word is *Luís*, the character's name. I also see clue words *want the biggest part in the school play*. There are details in the story that tell why Luís wants the biggest part. I'll look for those details, and I'll write about why Luís wants that part.
- In the next question, I see the clue words *What happened* so this question asks about an event in the story. Some other important clue words are *during Jennifer's music lesson*. I'll write about something that happened when Jennifer was having her music lesson.

Answering the Question

Question 1 Duplicate pages A2, A16, and A17 and distribute pages A2 and A16. Have children read "The Big Cleanup." (You might want children to number the paragraphs.) Explain that page A2 shows the four steps children should use to answer the questions. Work with children to answer question 1, a short-answer question, using the steps.

Steps for Answering Open-Response Questions

1 READ THE QUESTION

Have children find the clue words in the question. Use the prompts below.
- Circle the clue words that tell you if the question is asking about characters and events. *[Chela, Mom, and Mr. Naylor]*
- Circle the clue word that tells you what you will write about Chela, Mom, and Mr. Naylor. *[alike]*
- What does this question ask you to write about? **[ways in which Chela, Mom, and Mr. Naylor are alike]**

---

more ➡

Understanding Stories (continued)

② SEARCH AND FIND

Have children look at the story for details that answer the question. Use the prompt below.

- Which details help you know how Chela, Mom, and Mr. Naylor are alike? Underline these details. **[Children should underline paragraphs 1 and 3, sentence 1 of paragraph 4, and the first three sentences of paragraph 8.]**

③ GET READY TO WRITE

Work with children to make notes, listing details from the story. On the board, model making a list of details that answer the question.

[Ways Chela, Mom, and Mr. Naylor are alike

– upset that the beach is dirty

– want to help clean it up]

④ WRITE YOUR ANSWER

Review the guidelines under Step 4 on page A2. Tell children to follow them when writing their answers. Show children how to use their list of details to write a clear and complete response to question 1. Write the sample answer on the board. **[*Sample high-scoring response:* Chela, Mom, and Mr. Naylor are alike because they all feel the beach is too dirty. They are all ready to help clean it up.]** Ask children to compare the answer to each point in the guidelines.

Question 2 Work with children to use Steps 1–3 to answer question 2 on page A16. Explain that this is a long-answer question, which requires children to write more. When you reach Step 4, distribute page A17, which shows sample answers for question 2. Answers to Steps 1–4 are given below.

① READ THE QUESTION

[Children should circle *Chela and Mom do* (clue words for characters and events) and *to get the beach cleaned up* (clue words for what to write about). The question asks them to tell what Chela and Mom do to get the beach cleaned up.]

② SEARCH AND FIND

[Children should underline paragraphs 5, 7, and 9; and details in sentence 1 in paragraph 10.]

more ➡

Understanding Stories *(continued)*

❸ GET READY TO WRITE

[What Chela and Mom do
– talk to neighbors in six other cabins
– ask them to help clean up the beach
– divide up beach into seven parts
– one part for each family to clean
– work hard all day on their part until beach clean]

❹ WRITE YOUR ANSWER

[Children should circle paragraph B.] These scoring analyses explain the score of each sample answer.

Sample Answer A This response tells one detail about what Chela and Mom do to get the beach cleaned up. (*Chela and Mom talk to the neighbors, and the beach gets cleaned up*). However, the student doesn't mention any details about Chela and Mom dividing the beach into seven parts or working hard cleaning it themselves. Also, the student includes details about how dirty the beach is that don't answer the question.

Sample Answer B This top-scoring response provides a complete, accurate description of what Chela and Mom do to get the beach cleaned up. The student tells about Chela and Mom asking neighbors in six other cabins to help, dividing the beach into seven parts, and working hard all day cleaning their part.

Try It Out

Students can use the Practice Tests on pages A18–A23 for more practice answering open-response questions.

Name _____

Understanding Stories

The Big Cleanup

Q 1
1   Chela looked at the shores of Pine Lake and sighed. "It's so dirty, Mom!" she said.

2   Mom looked at the lake. The sandy beach was full of soda cans, plastic bags, candy wrappers, and other trash.

Q 1
3   "Maybe we could clean up the beach," Chela said.

4   "That's a good idea," said Mom. "We're going to be here for a week. What could we do to get the job done?"

Q 2
5   Chela pointed to the other six cabins on the shore. "Maybe we could talk to our neighbors," she said. "We could all clean up the beach together."

6   "That's a great idea!" said Mom. "Let's ask them."

Q 2
7   Together Chela and Mom knocked on every door. All the neighbors liked Chela's idea.

Q 1
8   "Once this beach was always clean," said Mr. Naylor. "With so many visitors, it gets dirty. I'll help clean it up." People in the other cabins said the same thing.

Q 2
9   Chela and Mom divided up the beach into seven parts. Each family cleaned up their part.

10   After working hard all day, the neighbors had a big campfire on the beach. Chela looked at the clean brown sand and the shiny black pebbles on the beach.

11   Mom smiled and squeezed Chela's hand. "It looks like your big cleanup was a big success," she said.

Answer these questions about the story above.

SHORT RESPONSE **1.** How are Chela, Mom, and Mr. Naylor alike? Use details from the story in your answer.

LONG RESPONSE **2.** What do Chela and Mom do to get the beach cleaned up? Use details from the story.

See page i for notes about the annotations and ideas for using the page.

Name _____

Understanding Stories

 LONG RESPONSE Read these answers to question 2 on page A16. Circle the answer that tells all the things that Chela and Mom do to get the beach cleaned up.

A The beach is really dirty. It has soda cans, candy wrappers, and other trash on it. Lots of people visit the beach. That's why it is so dirty. Chela and Mom talk to the neighbors, and the beach gets cleaned up.

B Chela and Mom ask their neighbors in six other cabins to help clean up the beach. Chela and Mom divide the beach into seven parts, one for each family to clean up. Then they work hard all day cleaning their part. Because Chela and Mom do these things, the beach gets cleaned up.

Name _____

Read the story "Belling the Cat," and then answer Numbers 1 and 2.

Belling the Cat

The mice had a problem. The cat was always looking around, ready to jump on them. She was very quiet and good at hiding. She sneaked up on the mice without a sound. The mice never saw her until she was right upon them.

The mice were afraid of the cat. They decided that something had to be done about her. So the mice held a meeting to find a way to solve this problem with the cat.

One by one, mice stood up to share their ideas. Each time, the other mice gave a reason why that plan would not work.

Finally, a little mouse stood up and said, "I have a plan that will surely work. All we have to do is hang a bell around the cat's neck. When we hear the bell, we will know the cat is close. Then we will have time to run for our lives."

All the mice thought about the plan. They were surprised that no one had thought of it before. The mice thought that their problem with the cat was over. They danced with joy.

"Wait a minute," an old mouse called out. "That plan is a good one, but I have one question. Who is going to hang the bell around the cat's neck?"

The Lesson It is one thing to say that something should be done. It is another thing to be the one to do it.

Go On

1 The cat is very quiet. Why is that a problem for the mice? Use details from the story to support your answer.

SHORT SPONSE

_____

_____

_____

_____

2 Why might the little mouse's plan not work? Use details from the story to support your answer.

LONG SPONSE

_____

_____

_____

_____

_____

_____

_____

Read the story "Meet Beatrix Potter," and then answer Numbers 1 and 2.

Meet Beatrix Potter

You may have read <u>The Tale of Peter Rabbit</u>. Peter gets into trouble. He sneaks into Mr. McGregor's garden. In the end, though, Peter gets back home safely.

Beatrix Potter first wrote this tale as a letter. She mailed the story and pictures to a sick child. Later, the story became a book. <u>The Tale of Peter Rabbit</u> is still well liked today.

Beatrix Potter lived in England. While she was growing up, her family often took long trips. They went to English lakes. On these trips, Beatrix spent many hours drawing and painting. She made pictures of lakes and streams, fields and trees. Her love for the country shows in her books.

Beatrix also loved animals. When she was a child, she had many pets. She had a rabbit named Peter. She had mice and frogs. She even had a hedgehog! Beatrix made many drawings of her pets. Her love for animals shows in her books.

Beatrix Potter wrote over twenty books and painted the pictures for them too. She wanted her books to be small. She wanted them to fit in a child's hands.

Children everywhere remember Beatrix for the characters in her books. Do you know Peter, Flopsy, Mopsy, and Cotton-tail? What about Squirrel Nutkin and Benjamin Bunny? All these characters can be found in Beatrix Potter's books.

Go On

Name _____

1 What size did Beatrix Potter want her books to be? Why? Use details from the story to support your answer.

SHORT SPONSE

_____

_____

_____

_____

2 What did Beatrix Potter like to write books about? Use details from the story to support your answer.

LONG SPONSE

_____

_____

_____

_____

_____

_____

_____

Name _____

Read the story "How a Mosquito Grows Up," and then answer Numbers 1 and 2.

How a Mosquito Grows Up

Mosquitoes fly around. They can bite you. Mosquito bites make itchy, red bumps on your skin. Did you know that when a mosquito is first born, it cannot bite you? A young mosquito does not even have wings.

Most mosquito eggs hatch in water. When a mosquito comes out of the egg, it is a little black worm called a larva. The larva floats up near the surface of the water. It breathes through a tube that it sticks out of the water. The larva eats little water plants and grows bigger.

After the larva eats and grows bigger, it turns into a pupa. A mosquito pupa has a hard black shell. The pupa stays in the water and does not eat.

When the mosquito comes out of the shell, it is all grown up. It has wings and tries to fly away. You had better watch out! This mosquito might be the one that wants to bite you!

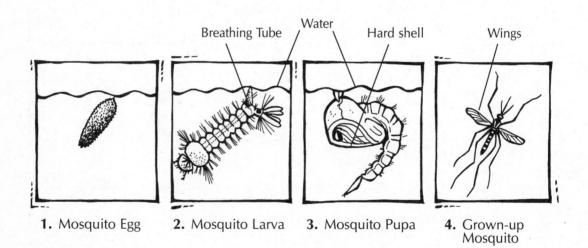

1. Mosquito Egg   **2.** Mosquito Larva   **3.** Mosquito Pupa   **4.** Grown-up Mosquito

Go On

1 Look at picture 2 on page A22. How does the tube help the larva breathe? Use details from the story to support your answer.

SHORT
RESPONSE

_____

_____

_____

2 Would you find more mosquitoes in a swamp or in a desert? Use details from the story to support your answer.

LONG
RESPONSE

_____

_____

_____

_____

_____

_____

_____

PART B

Support for Writing Tests

Reading the Prompt:
Instruction and Prompts

Elaboration Strategies Practice

Benchmark Papers, Rubrics, and Analyses

Reading a Personal Narrative Prompt

Discuss the characteristics of a successful personal narrative. Use page 152 in Theme 5 of the *Houghton Mifflin Reading Teacher's Edition* or page 67 of the *Houghton Mifflin English* pupil edition.

Reading the Prompt

Explain that writing prompts have clue words that tell the kind of paper to write as well as some ideas about what to put in the paper. Write this prompt on the board, and read it aloud.

> Think about a time when you celebrated a holiday. What did you do? Write a story telling all about what happened when you celebrated a holiday. Be sure to write about the events in your story in detail.

Planning a Response

In the prompt, circle the words *a story, what happened,* and *a time when you.* Explain that these words are important because they give clues about the kind of paper to write—a personal narrative. Remind children that a personal narrative is a story about themselves, telling something that really happened. Use the Think Aloud to model how to analyze the prompt further.

Think Aloud

What does this prompt tell me to put in my personal narrative? I see the words *celebrated a holiday.* This is the topic that I should write about, so I'll underline it. Now I will think of something I have done that fits this topic. I could write about Thanksgiving at my grandparents' house, but I think I'll write about riding my bike in the Independence Day parade. I will write details about how I got ready for the parade, what I saw before and during the parade, and how excited I felt.

Draw this chart, including only the labels. Together, fill in the information provided in the prompt and Think Aloud, shown in italics below. Then brainstorm and record details telling what might have happened first, next, and last. Be sure to answer the questions *who, what, why, when,* and *where,* using exact details. Sample details are in brackets.

Kind of Paper	*Personal Narrative*	
Topic	*what happened when you celebrated a holiday* [rode my bike in Independence Day parade]	
First	[decorated my bike in red, white, and blue; put little flags on handlebars]	
Next	[went to the park at 9:00 in the morning; saw lots of people; heard a band playing; smelled hot dogs and popcorn]	
Last	[rode in the parade; loud drums; cheering people; colorful balloons; felt excited]	

Try It Together

Duplicate and distribute Blackline Master B3. Work with children to complete the page. For more practice with personal narrative prompts, use the first prompt on both pages B17 and B18.

Name _____

Reading a Personal Narrative Prompt

Work with your teacher and classmates.
Read this prompt and fill in the chart.

People have favorite places they like to
visit. Write a story telling all about what
happened when you went to a favorite place.
Include exact details.

Test Tip
Look for clue words
that tell the kind
of paper to write
and the topic.

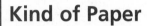

Kind of Paper	
Topic	
First	
Next	
Last	

Reading a Story Prompt

Discuss the characteristics of a successful story. Use page 42 in Theme 1 of the *Houghton Mifflin Reading Teacher's Edition* or page 139 of the *Houghton Mifflin English* pupil edition.

Reading the Prompt

Explain that writing prompts have clue words that tell the kind of paper to write as well as some ideas about what to put in the paper. Point out that the writer must often make up any parts of the story that are not given in the prompt and put them in his or her paper. Write this prompt on the board or chart paper, and read it aloud.

> Pretend that one summer morning two friends find an unusual shovel at the beach. Write a story about what happens after the friends find the shovel.

Planning a Response

Circle the words *Pretend* and *a story* in the prompt. Explain that these words are important because they give clues about the kind of paper to write—a story. Review the key parts of a story: characters, setting, the problem and how it is solved, and a beginning, middle, and end. Read the Think Aloud to model how to analyze the prompt. As you do, underline clue words for the key parts in the prompt.

Think Aloud

I see the words *Pretend* and *story* in this prompt, so I know I will write a story that I make up. Now I will look for what this prompt tells me to put in my story. I see the words *two friends,* so they must be the characters. I also see the words *summer morning* and *beach*. These must name the setting. The prompt tells me that the friends find an *unusual shovel*. This isn't really a problem, so I must make up a problem and tell how it is solved. I will write a story about two friends who have a problem after they find an unusual shovel on a beach.

Draw and display a chart like this one, including only the labels. Explain that completing the chart will help organize information for writing a story. First, fill in information from the prompt, shown in italics below. Together, brainstorm and choose ideas for the problem and how it is solved. Fill in the chart with this information. Sample ideas are shown in brackets.

Kind of Paper *Story*	
Characters, Setting, Problem, and Solution	
Beginning	*two friends at the beach one summer morning; find an unusual shovel* [Handle looks like bone; friends begin digging.]
Middle	[Big dog sees shovel; he thinks it is a bone, takes shovel, and runs into water.]
End	[Two friends tell lifeguard; lifeguard catches dog, gives dog a biscuit, returns shovel.]

Try It Together

Duplicate and distribute Blackline Master B5. Work with children to complete the page. For more practice with story prompts, use the third prompt on page B17 and on page B18.

Name _____

Reading a Story Prompt

Work with your teacher and classmates.
Read this prompt. Fill in the chart.

Pretend that one afternoon Jake visits a
toy store. He sees a train and hears its
whistle blow. All of a sudden, he finds himself
on a real train. Write a story telling all about
what happens to Jake on the train ride.

> **Test Tip**
> Look for clue words
> that tell the kind of
> paper and the key
> parts to put in it.

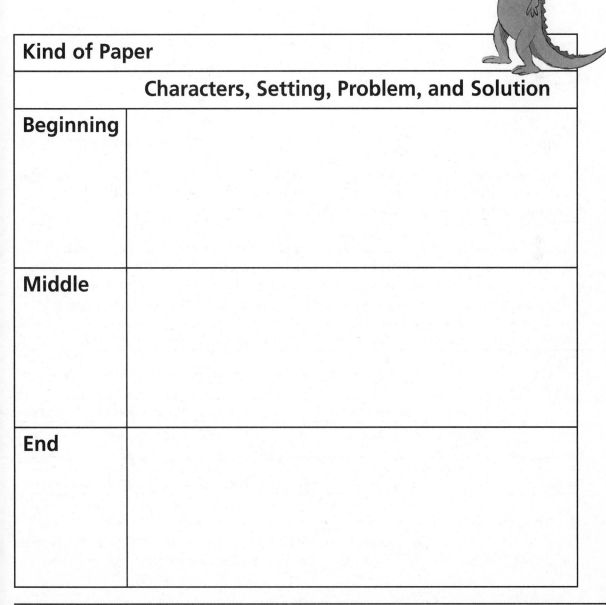

Kind of Paper	
Characters, Setting, Problem, and Solution	
Beginning	
Middle	
End	

Reading an Instructions Prompt

Discuss the characteristics of a successful instructions paper. Use page 326 in Theme 6 of the *Houghton Mifflin Reading Teacher's Edition* or page 209 of the *Houghton Mifflin English* pupil edition.

Reading the Prompt

Explain that writing prompts have clue words that tell the kind of paper to write as well as some ideas about what to put in the paper. Write this prompt on the board, and read it aloud.

> Think of one activity you do in your classroom. Write a paper for your teacher explaining all about how you do this activity. Be sure to explain each step fully.

Planning a Response

Circle *explaining* and *how you do this activity* in the prompt. Explain that these words tell the kind of paper to write—instructions. Review the key parts of instructions: topic, materials, order words, steps, and details. Use the Think Aloud to model analyzing the prompt.

Think Aloud

I will look for what this prompt tells me to put in my instructions. I see the words *one activity you do in your classroom*. This must be the topic, so I will underline it. I need to choose an activity in my classroom that I know how to do. I could write about how to do a writing conference with a classmate or how to use the computer. I think I'll write about how to get ready for lunch. I do that every day.

Draw a chart like this one, including only the labels. Explain that completing the chart will help organize information for writing an instructions paper. First, fill in the information from the prompt and Think Aloud, shown in italics. Together, brainstorm and choose materials, order words, steps, and the details for each step. Sample answers are shown in brackets.

Kind of Paper *Instructions*		Topic *activity you do in your classroom* [getting ready for lunch]
Materials [lunch, milk money]		
Order Words	Steps	Details
First	1 [Put away all work.]	[Put books in desk; make everything neat.]
[Next]	2 [Wash hands at sink.]	[Use soap; dry hands well.]
[Then]	3 [Get lunch and milk money from locker.]	[Do not run; talk quietly.]
[Last]	4 [Line up at the classroom door.]	[Wait until all are ready; do not push.]

Try It Together

Duplicate and distribute Blackline Master B7. Work with children to complete the page. For more practice with instructions, use the fifth prompt on page B17 and the fourth prompt on page B18.

Name _____

Reading an Instructions Prompt

Work with your teacher and classmates.
Read this prompt. Fill in the chart.

> **Test Tip**
> Look for clue words that tell the kind of paper and the topic.

Think of one group game, such as tag, that you know how to play. Write a paper for your teacher explaining all about how you play this game. Explain each step so that someone else would know how to play it.

Kind of Paper		Topic	
Materials			
Order Words	**Steps**		**Details**
	1		
	2		
	3		
	4		

Reading a Description Prompt

Discuss what makes a successful description. Use page 154 in Theme 2 of the *Houghton Mifflin Reading Teacher's Edition* or page 271 of the *Houghton Mifflin English* pupil edition.

Reading a Prompt

Explain that writing prompts have clue words that tell the kind of paper to write as well as some ideas about what to put in the paper. Write this prompt on the board, and read it aloud.

> Think about a place at your school where you go for recess. Write a description of this place. Include details that use at least three of your five senses.

Planning a Response

In the prompt, circle the word *description*. Explain that this word is important because it gives a clue about what kind of paper to write—a description. Remind students that a description helps their readers see, feel, hear, taste, and smell what they are writing about. Use the Think Aloud to model how to analyze the prompt further.

Think Aloud

I will look for what this prompt tells me to put in my description. I see the words *a place at your school where you go for recess.* This is the topic that I should write about, so I'll underline it. Where do we have recess? We usually go to the playground, so I will write about that. I'll write about how it looks, sounds, and feels.

Draw this chart, including only the labels. Together, fill in the information in the prompt and the Think Aloud, shown in italics below. Then brainstorm and record details telling more about the place students go for recess. Be sure to brainstorm sense words and details for at least three of the five senses. Ideas for prompting students are shown in brackets.

Kind of Paper	*Description*
Topic	*place at your school where you go for recess* [playground]
How It Looks	[What equipment is there: swings? slides?] [What is on the ground: pavement? grass? dirt?]
How It Sounds	[What sounds do students make? teachers?] [What sounds does the equipment make?]
How It Feels	[What does the slide feel like? the swings? other equipment?] [What does the ground feel like? the air?]
How It Tastes	
How It Smells	

Try It Together

Duplicate and distribute Blackline Master B9. Work with students to complete this page. For more practice with description prompts, use the fifth prompt on page B18.

Name _____

Reading a Description Prompt

Work with your teacher and classmates.
Read this prompt and fill in the chart.

Test Tip
Look for clue words that tell the kind of paper to write and the topic.

What is a rainy day like? Write a description of a rainy day. Be sure to describe your topic in detail.

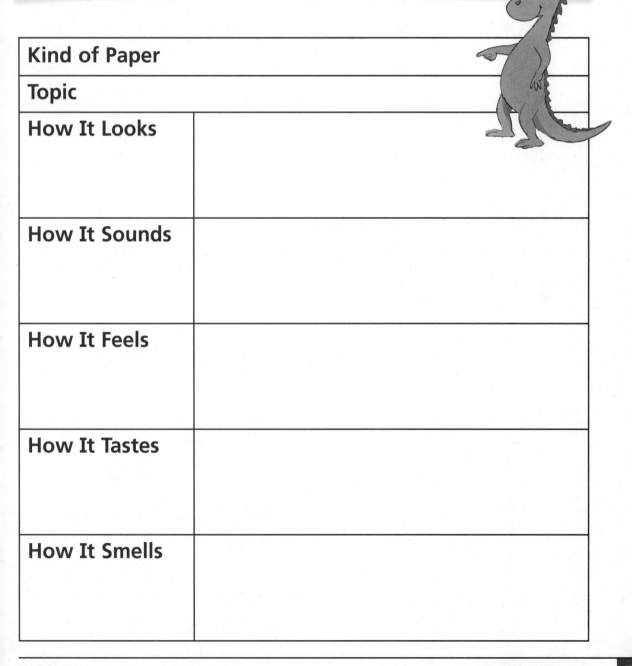

Kind of Paper	
Topic	
How It Looks	
How It Sounds	
How It Feels	
How It Tastes	
How It Smells	

Reading an Opinion/Explanation Prompt

Note: Sometimes an opinion essay is referred to as an explanation or a personal essay.
Discuss what makes a successful opinion essay. Use page 345 of the *Houghton Mifflin English* pupil edition. For students using *Houghton Mifflin Reading,* use these lessons in the *Teacher's Edition*: Writing Skills: An Opinion Paragraph on page 151M of Theme 5 and Writing Skills: A Paragraph That Explains on page 325M of Theme 6.

Reading the Prompt

Explain that writing prompts have clue words that tell the kind of paper to write as well as some ideas for what to put in the paper. Write this prompt on the board. Read it aloud.

> Why do you like summer? Write an essay for your teacher explaining why you like summer. Be sure to write about your reasons in detail.

Planning a Response

Circle the words *explaining* and *why* in the prompt. Explain that these words give clues about the kind of paper to write—an opinion essay. Review the key parts of an opinion essay: it explains your feelings about a topic; it gives reasons to explain why you feel as you do; it gives examples to support each reason. Use the Think Aloud to model how to analyze the prompt further.

....

Think Aloud

I will underline the topic that this prompt names. I see the words *why you like summer*. That must be the topic. I will write a paper with reasons and examples that explain why I like summer. Does the prompt tell me the audience? I see the words *for your teacher,* so I will write for my teacher.

....

Draw and display a chart like this one, including only the labels. First, fill in information from the prompt, shown in italics below. Together, brainstorm, choose, and record two reasons for liking summer. Then think of and record examples to support the reasons. Samples are shown in brackets.

Kind of Paper *Opinion essay*	
Topic *why you like summer*	
Audience *your teacher*	
Reason 1 [have more time to play]	**Reason 2** [can go to the beach a lot]
Example 1 [school vacation]	**Example 1** [go every day it doesn't rain]
Example 2 [can play outdoors after dinner]	**Example 2** [swim and play in the sand]

Try It Together

Duplicate and distribute Blackline Master B11. Work with children to complete the page. For more practice with opinion prompts, use the second prompt on both page B17 and page B18.

Name _____

Reading an Opinion/Explanation Prompt

Work with your teacher and classmates.
Read this prompt. Fill in the chart.

Test Tip
Look for clue words
that tell the kind
of paper, the topic,
and the audience.

Think about why you like Saturdays.
Write an essay for your teacher explaining
why you like Saturdays. Be sure to include both
reasons and examples to support your reasons.

Kind of Paper	
Topic	
Audience	
Reason 1	**Reason 2**
Example 1	**Example 1**
Example 2	**Example 2**

Reading a Persuasive Prompt

Discuss the characteristics of a persuasive essay. Use pages 362–363 of the *Houghton Mifflin English* pupil edition. For students using *Houghton Mifflin Reading,* use Writing Skills: Writing to Persuade on pages 367M–367N in Theme 3 of the *Teacher's Edition.*

Reading the Prompt

Explain that writing prompts have clue words that tell the kind of paper to write as well as ideas about what to put in the paper. Write this prompt on the board and read it aloud.

> Your principal has money for a class cooking project or an art project. Write an essay for your principal telling which project you would like to do. Give reasons that will persuade him or her to accept your choice. Be sure to write about your reasons in detail.

Planning a Response

Circle *an essay, reasons, persuade,* and *your choice* in the prompt. Explain that these words give clues about the kind of paper to write—a persuasive essay. Remind children that when they write reasons to convince someone to agree with their choice, they are writing to persuade. Tell students that a prompt might ask them to write a persuasive letter instead of an essay. Use the Think Aloud to model how to analyze the prompt.

Think Aloud

I will look for and underline what this prompt tells me to put in my persuasive essay. I see the words *a class cooking project or an art project* and *which project you would like to do.* These words tell me to choose a goal. I'll choose this goal: we should do a cooking project. The words *your principal* tell the audience. So I will write reasons to persuade my principal that our class should do a cooking project.

Draw and display a web like this one, including only the labels. Then fill in information from the prompt and Think Aloud, shown in italics below. Together, brainstorm reasons for doing a cooking project and choose two. Have children tell more about each reason by providing two supporting facts or examples. Sample answers are shown in brackets.

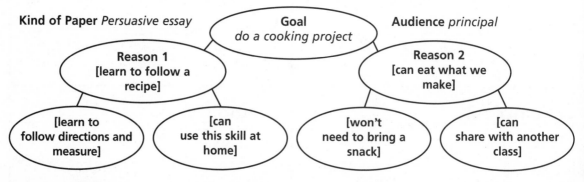

Try It Together

Duplicate and distribute Blackline Master B13. Work with children to complete the page. For more practice with persuasive prompts, use the fourth prompt on page B17.

Name _____

Reading a Persuasive Prompt

Work with your teacher and classmates.
Read this prompt. Fill in the chart.

Test Tip
Look for clue words
that tell the kind
of paper, the goal,
and the audience.

Your parents are making new rules for
your family. Think of one rule that would be
good for your family. Write an essay for your
parents, telling one good rule for your family.
Give reasons to persuade them to accept your
choice.

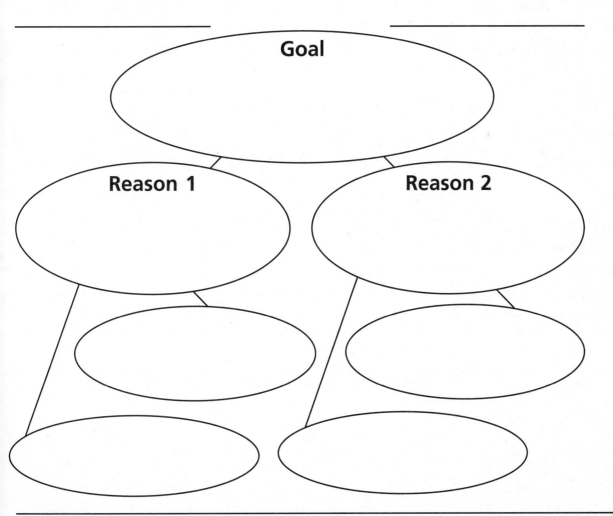

Kind of Paper   **Audience**

_____   _____

Goal

Reason 1   Reason 2

Blackline Master   **B13**

Reading Prompts

Reading a Prompt: Finding the Kind of Writing

Review with children that the papers they write for a test must fit the topic and the kind of writing given in a prompt. On the board, write these labels: *Description, Personal Narrative, Story, Instructions, Opinion Essay,* and *Persuasive Essay.* Explain to children that while they might use different kinds of writing to tell about similar topics, writing prompts on tests tell them the kind of writing they must use. Explain that certain words will give clues about the kind of writing they should use.

Duplicate and distribute page B15. Read aloud the three shortened example prompts at the top of the page. Use the Think Aloud to model finding the topic and kind of writing.

Think Aloud

I see the word *garden* in Examples *A, B,* and *C,* so gardens must be the topic of each prompt. Now what do the clue words tell me about the kinds of writing I must do? In Example *A,* I'll circle the words *Write a story.* I'll also circle the words *what you did.* These words tell me to write a story about what I actually did, so I'll write a personal narrative. In Example *B,* I'll circle the words *explaining* and *how you would plant.* These words tell me to write an instructions paper. In Example *C,* I'll circle the words *why you would like.* These words tell me to write an opinion essay.

Planning a Response

Together, fill in a chart like the one below for each of the prompt parts. First, discuss the key parts of each kind of writing. Then brainstorm ideas for each key part and choose some to put in the chart. Sample ideas are shown in brackets.

Example A Personal Narrative	**Topic** *what you did in a garden* [getting vegetables]
	First, Next, Last [picking vegetables; bringing them to the house; making salad]
	Details [First, I picked crisp green lettuce, juicy ripe tomatoes, and red, orange, and green peppers; next, I carried the vegetables in a basket to the house; finally, I made a salad in a wooden bowl.]
Example B Instructions	**Topic** *how to plant a garden*
	Materials [seeds, spade, water]
	Steps [dig a hole, plant the seed, water it]
	Details [make hole the right depth for each kind of seed; add plant food; water once a day]
Example C Opinion	**Topic** *why you would like caring for a garden*
	Reasons [get vegetables to eat; get flowers to look at]
	Examples [eating crisp green lettuce, ripe red tomatoes, and red, orange, and green peppers; looking at red and purple tulips, black and yellow sunflowers]

Try It Together

Have children complete the rest of pages B15 and B16. You may want to specify one or more of these prompts for which you want children to plan a response.

Reading Prompts

Think and Discuss Read and discuss clue words in these parts of prompts.

Test Tip
Read every prompt very carefully.

A. Write a story telling all about what you did in a garden.

B. Write an essay for your teacher explaining all about how you would plant a garden.

C. Write an essay for your teacher telling why you would like caring for a garden.

Try It Out

Read the prompts below and on page B16. For each prompt, draw a line under the clue words that tell about the topic. Circle the clue words that tell about the kind of writing.

Pretend that a friend is given three wishes by a little elf. Write a story telling all about the friend's wishes and what happens. Be sure to write about the events of your story in detail.

Your family is planning a trip to a faraway city. You can travel by plane, train, bus, car, or boat. Write an essay for your parents telling the one way you would most like to travel to this faraway city. Give reasons for your choice. Be sure to write about your reasons in detail.

Name _____

Writing Prompts

Think about why you like starting a new school year. Write an essay for your teacher explaining why you like starting a new school year. Support your reasons with examples.

Pretend that Sam went to the circus and suddenly found himself chosen as the circus ringmaster for that day. Write a story telling about Sam's day as ringmaster at the circus. Tell about a problem and how it was solved.

Your teacher wants to turn a children's book into a play that your class will perform and asks you to suggest one good book. Write an essay for your teacher. In this essay tell what one book you think would make a good play. Give reasons that will persuade your teacher to accept your choice. Include facts and examples to support your reasons.

What is your favorite food? Write a description of your favorite food. Include details that use at least three of your five senses.

Think of a time when you visited relatives or when they came to visit you. Write a story telling all about what happened. Be sure to write about the events in your story in detail.

Name _____

Writing Prompts *(continued)*

What was the best birthday party you ever had or ever went to? Write a story for your classmates telling all about what happened at this birthday party. Be sure to write about the events in your story in detail.

Why do you like indoor recess? Write an essay for your teacher explaining why you like indoor recess. Tell at least two reasons, and include examples to support each reason.

Pretend that a friend of yours is an inventor. Your friend has just invented a wonderful machine that can help people. What does this machine do? Write a story telling all about your friend's wonderful machine. Include details about characters, setting, a problem, and how the problem is solved.

You think that you are old enough to be allowed to do one certain activity. Write an essay for your parents to convince them that you are old enough to be allowed to do this one activity. Include facts and examples to support your reasons.

How do you clean up your bedroom? Write an essay for your teacher explaining all about how you clean up your bedroom. Be sure to explain each step fully so that someone else would know how to do it.

Name _____

Writing Prompts *(continued)*

Everyone has seen something interesting or amazing. Write a story telling all about a time when you saw something interesting or amazing. Be sure to write about the events of your story in detail.

Why do you like your house? Write an essay for your teacher explaining why you like your house. Be sure to write about your reasons in detail.

Pretend that your friend has a pet dinosaur. Write a story telling all about what your friend and the pet dinosaur do together. Tell about a problem and how it is solved.

Think about how to feed a pet. Write an essay for your teacher explaining all about how you feed a pet. Explain each step so that someone else would know how to do it.

What is your bedroom like? Write a description of your bedroom for a friend. Include details that use at least three of your five senses.

Name _____

Using Exact Details

Rewrite each sentence. Write an exact detail from
the box to take the place of the underlined words.

a beautiful ocean beach	the best day of the summer
shells and crabs	a huge castle with towers

Example   My family went to <u>a nice place</u>.

My family went to a beautiful ocean beach.

1. Mia built <u>a big building</u>.

_____

_____

_____

2. We found <u>cool stuff</u>.

_____

_____

3. It was <u>a fun time</u>!

_____

_____

With a classmate, think of exact details to replace the
underlined words in the sentence below. Then rewrite
the sentence on another sheet of paper.

4. We ate <u>good food</u> at the beach.

Name _____

Asking and Answering Questions

Read each sentence. Then answer the questions, using details from the box. Rewrite each sentence, adding the new details.

quietly	for a music show	spotted
last night	on the rock	my dad

Example The snow fell. **When** did the snow fall?
How did the snow fall?

Last night the snow fell quietly.

1. A toad hopped. What did the toad look like?

Where did it hop?

_____

- -

_____

2. My mom sang. Whom did she sing with?

Why did she sing?

_____

- -

_____

With a classmate, ask questions about each sentence below. Then add details that answer the questions and rewrite each sentence on another sheet of paper.

3. One balloon floated.

4. A train stopped.

5. The dog barked.

Name _____

Using Sensory Words

Complete and rewrite each sentence, using sensory words from the box.

See	Hear	Feel	Taste	Smell
red	barking	soft	sour	smoky
tiny	loud	smooth	juicy	fresh
yellow	squeaky	bumpy	spicy	sweet

Example   A _____ dog ran past the _____ barn.

A barking dog ran past the red barn.

1. The _____ hay smelled _____.

_____

_____

2. A _____ tractor scared the _____ bunnies.

_____

_____

3. Sue and I picked _____, _____ berries.

_____

_____

With a classmate, add sensory words to these sentences and rewrite them on another sheet of paper.

4. At the cookout, tables were set up near the fence.

5. We had bread, corn, and watermelon for lunch.

Name _____

Using on, at, in, and with to Add Details

Rewrite each sentence, adding a detail from the box to fill in the blank.

at the park	on first base
in his glove	with her bat

Example We played baseball _____.

We played baseball at the park.

1. Meg hit the ball _____.

_____

_____

2. Ben stepped _____.

_____

_____

3. He caught the ball _____.

_____

_____

4–6. Read this paragraph. With a classmate, think of details that begin with on, at, in, or with to fill in the blanks. Rewrite the paragraph on another sheet of paper, adding the details.

Our family went to a funny restaurant _____. We had a big table _____. There were silly pictures _____.

Name _____

Using Exact Nouns

Write an exact noun from the box to take the place of the underlined noun in each sentence.

sharks	teacher	computer
oceans	books	

Example   I am writing a report about <u>fish</u>.   *sharks*

_____

1. A <u>person</u> helped me find facts.   _____

_____

2. She gave me <u>things</u> to read.   _____

_____

3. I used a <u>machine</u> to get pictures.   _____

_____

4. I read that sharks live in <u>water</u>.   _____

5–10. With a classmate, think of exact nouns to take the place of the underlined nouns below. Then rewrite the paragraph on another sheet of paper.

Once upon a time, there was a <u>person</u> who lived in a big <u>building</u>. One day he went for a walk with his <u>pet</u>. They walked to a <u>place</u> and saw a big <u>thing</u> near a tree. He wondered if <u>animals</u> lived there.

Name _____

Using Exact Verbs

Write an exact verb from the box to take the place of the underlined verb in each sentence.

hiked	dashed	whispered
hid	spotted	

Example   Diego and Gina <u>walked</u> up the trail. hiked

_____

1. "Look by that stream," Gina <u>said</u>. _____

_____

2. She had <u>seen</u> a little deer. _____

_____

3. The deer suddenly <u>moved</u> away. _____

_____

4. It <u>went</u> behind a tree. _____

5–10. With a classmate, think of exact verbs to take the place of the underlined verbs below. Then rewrite the paragraph on another sheet of paper.

I <u>like</u> my new computer game! A spaceship <u>goes</u> across the screen. Space rocks <u>come</u> toward you. The captain <u>talks</u> if a rock gets too close. The rocks <u>break</u> if you hit them. The goal is to <u>get</u> on all of the planets.

Name _____

Using Exact Adjectives

Replace each underlined adjective with an exact adjective from the box.

beautiful	brief	tiny
colorful	huge	

 beautiful
Example   We have a ~~nice~~ clubhouse.

1. We built it in a <u>big</u> tree.

2. The clubhouse has a <u>small</u> door with a peephole.

3. The windows have <u>bright</u> curtains.

4. We have a <u>short</u> club meeting every afternoon.

With a classmate, think of exact adjectives to take the place of the underlined adjectives below. Then rewrite the sentences on another sheet of paper.

5. Our family took a <u>good</u> trip.

6. We went on some <u>fun</u> rides.

7. The <u>fast</u> roller coaster was my favorite.

8. I had a <u>cold</u> drink at the park.

Grade 2

Using Adverbs

Some **adverbs** tell how actions were done.
Write an adverb from the box to tell how
each underlined action was done.

gracefully	proudly	gently
slowly	quietly	

Example   The pony <u>jumped</u> ____ over the gate.   gracefully

1. Chen <u>smiled</u> ____ at his pony.

2. It <u>walked</u> ____ around the ring.

3. Chen ____ <u>patted</u> his pony.

4. He <u>whispered</u> ____ to the pony.

With a classmate, add an adverb to each sentence
below to tell how the underlined action was done.
Rewrite the sentences on another sheet of paper.

5. We <u>ran</u> to the ticket booth.

6. Mom <u>asked</u> for six circus tickets.

7. The lion tamer <u>moved</u>.

8. The seals <u>barked</u>.

Name _____

Using Similes

Rewrite each sentence. Use a simile from the box to take the place of the underlined word or words.

as swiftly as a rabbit	like a howling wolf
like twinkling stars	as icy as an igloo

Example   She ran <u>quickly</u>.

  She ran as swiftly as a rabbit.

1. The alarm sounded <u>loud</u>.

_____

_____

2. My feet felt <u>cold</u>.

_____

_____

3. The baby's eyes were <u>really bright</u>.

_____

_____

With a classmate, complete the similes in these sentences. Rewrite the sentences on another sheet of paper.

4. The clouds looked like _____.

5. Our classroom was as quiet as _____.

6. The man's voice sounds like _____.

Using Sound Words

Write a sound word from the box to name the sound each animal or thing makes.

hoot	peep	pop
crash	clang	hiss

Example   an owl hoot

1. a big bell   _____

_____

2. huge ocean waves _____

_____

3. baby birds   _____

_____

4. an angry snake   _____

_____

5. a breaking balloon _____

With a classmate, think of a sound word to complete each sentence below. Then rewrite each sentence on another sheet of paper.

6. The little kitten ____ to ask for milk.

7. The thunder ____ in the mountains.

8. The bee ____ as it landed on the flower.

Name _____

Beginning Sentences in Different Ways

Rewrite each sentence by changing the underlined words that begin it. Use words from the box.

John, Ed, Mary, and Rosa	All of the kids
They	The boys and girls

Example   The children went to the park.

John, Ed, Mary, and Rosa went to the park.

1. The children played on the swings.

_____

....

_____

2. The children zoomed down the slide.

_____

....

_____

3. The children had lots of fun.

_____

....

_____

4–5. With a classmate, make this paragraph more interesting by changing the beginnings of two sentences. Rewrite the paragraph on another sheet of paper.

My teacher took us to a science museum. My teacher showed us some dinosaurs. Juan and I saw dinosaur eggs. Juan and I touched a dinosaur bone.

Name _____

Using Different Kinds of Sentences

Rewrite each sentence. Change it to the kind of sentence named in ( ).

Example   Maria likes the zoo. (question)
  Does Maria like the zoo?

1. The animals are fun to watch. **(question)**

_____

_____

2. You should go to the zoo tomorrow. **(command)**

_____

_____

3. I think you will have a great time. (exclamation)

_____

_____

4–6. With a classmate, change or add to this paragraph so that it has telling sentences, a question, a command, and an exclamation. Rewrite the paragraph on another sheet of paper.

   Grandma gave me a puppy. I am teaching him tricks. Sparky can do a lot already. He can roll over and sit. He can even catch a ball. I think he is a smart puppy. I hope you can meet him soon.

Name _____

Personal Narrative   Score 4

Think about a time when you were surprised in a fun or exciting way. Write a story for your teacher about a time that you were surprised. Tell what happened and how you felt.

One boring summer day, I heard a loud knock on our front door. I ran to the kitchen and told my mom that someone was at the door. Mom quickly walked over and looked through the peephole. Aunt Mary had stopped by for a visit. Mom opened the door and invited her in. I said, "Hi, Aunt Mary," and gave her a hug. She was carrying something with a big blue blanket over it, and I wondered what it was.

My mom and dad made some coffee for Aunt Mary. I went to my room and thought about what she had brought with her. Maybe it was a suitcase.

Just then my mom called me, and I ran to the family room. Mom asked me what was different in the room. I looked around slowly and spotted something on the rug behind my dad's favorite chair. I saw a large metal cage with a beautiful green bird inside! I ran to Aunt Mary and thanked her for my wonderful new pet. That day I got my greatest surprise ever. It was a tiny green parakeet!

Name _____

Personal Narrative Score 3

Think about a time when you were surprised in a fun or exciting way. Write a story for your teacher about a time that you were surprised. Tell what happened and how you felt.

On my sixth birthday, I was really surprised! My family took me to a big theme park. We went in our camper. First, we went to a nice restaurant. When we got to the table, there were candy and balloons for me. The food was really good, and for dessert I got to decorate my own cupcake. After lunch we went over to the rides. My brother was very tired, so my mom took him back to the camper. My dad and I stayed and rode a lot of the rides. My favorite rides were The Mad Racer and The Twirly Top. That night my parents had another surprise for me. They gave me my birthday presents. My mom and dad gave me a doll, and my grandma gave me a sweatshirt and sweatpants. That was such a great birthday with so many surprises!

Name _____

Personal Narrative   Score 2

> Think about a time when you were surprised in a fun or exciting way. Write a story for your teacher about a time that you were surprised. Tell what happened and how you felt.

I was so surprised when she bought me a bike. I was surprised. It was a mountain bike with shocks on it to make your bike bounce up and down. It's cool. I also have in-line skates. I like playing outside. Sometimes I like to play basketball. I was really surprised with my bike. I love to do tricks on my bike. That's why I was so so so surprised. I love it.

Personal Narrative   `Score 1`

> Think about a time when you were surprised in a fun or exciting way. Write a story for your teacher about a time that you were surprised. Tell what happened and how you felt.

I like surprises. They are fun. I like games. I was surprised when my dad came home. He gave us presents. I got a game. It is a fun game. I like playing outside. I play tag with my friends at school. It is fun. I like soccer and kickball too.

Personal Narrative   `Unscorable`

Once upon a time, there was a little girl who loved to swim. Every day her mother took her to a nearby pond to swim. One day she was sitting by the pond when she saw a turtle. She said to the turtle, "You are so lucky that you are a turtle. You get to live in the pond and swim whenever you want. I wish I could be a turtle too." The turtle looked at the girl and said, "Your wish is granted." Then the girl became a turtle, and she lived happily ever after.

Personal Narrative

Score 4 The paper is focused on the topic and purpose given in the prompt. An interesting beginning grabs the reader's attention, and the end tells how the story worked out or how the writer felt. All events are relevant and are told in the correct order. Details and exact words are used throughout. Sentences are written in different ways and flow smoothly. Any mistakes do not distract.

Score 3 The paper is generally focused on the topic and purpose. The beginning could be more interesting, and the end may make the narrative feel somewhat unfinished. Some events may be unimportant, and more details and ideas are needed. More time clues may be needed. Word choice and sentence variety can be improved. The few mistakes do not affect understanding.

Score 2 The paper stays somewhat focused on the topic and purpose, but it may have many unrelated events and details. The beginning or ending may be unclear or missing. Many events may be missing or sequenced incorrectly. There are few details, and readers are left with many questions. Word choice is limited, and the paper lacks sentence variety. Some mistakes affect understanding.

Score 1 The paper barely focuses on the topic and purpose and is unorganized. Many events and details are unrelated, missing, or simply listed. There is no elaboration. There are few sentences, or they are short or unclear. Many mistakes affect understanding.

Unscorable The paper doesn't respond to the prompt, may be illegible, or is written in a foreign language. The writer may do nothing more than restate the prompt, or the response may not be a personal narrative.

Personal Narrative

Score 4 **Benchmark Paper** The writer stays clearly focused on writing a personal narrative that follows the topic given in the prompt. There is a strong organizational structure to the writing. The writer has included an interesting beginning, middle, and end and has also used many exact words (*peephole, invited, carrying, coffee, spotted*). The writer has provided strong support with enough specific details (*big blue blanket, large metal cage*) and description of each event to give readers a clear and concise picture of what happened. The writer has varied the beginnings of sentences so that the paper reads smoothly.

Score 3 **Benchmark Paper** The narrative stays focused on the appropriate type of writing and the prompt. There is a good organizational structure to this paper, and the writer walks the reader through the experience, step by step. The narrative includes a somewhat detailed account of the most important events of the birthday surprise, but more supporting elaboration regarding the rides and the gifts is needed. In some places (*nice restaurant, food, really good*), the writer could have used words that are more exact in order to create vivid images for the reader. Order words and transitional phrases (*First, After lunch, That night*) are used effectively and help the sentences flow smoothly. The writer has also varied sentence beginnings and types.

English **HM English PE:** pp. 71, 73, 74, 78 **TE:** pp. 71, 74, 78 **WP:** pp. 21, 23, 24 **SWT:** pp. B19, B20, B22, B23, B24, B25, B29, B30
Reading **HM Reading TE:** *2.1* p. 335N *2.2* pp. 151L, 153B, 153D, 153E **PB:** *2.1* p. 193 *2.2* p. 83 **SWT:** pp. B19, B20, B22, B23, B24, B25, B29, B30

Score 2 **Benchmark Paper** The writer stays somewhat focused on the prompt, but the paper does include some unrelated details. The narrative is not well-organized, and there is no distinguishable beginning, middle, or end. Most of the paper has very little supporting elaboration and detail. There is no explanation of whom *she* refers to or why the writer received the bike. Word choice is often vague (*It's cool, I love to do tricks . . .*), and the writer has used the word *surprised* four times. The paper is actually more a description of the bike than a personal narrative about the surprise of receiving it. The sentences are short and choppy.

English **HM English PE:** pp. 71, 72, 73, 74, 78 **TE:** pp. 71, 72, 74, 78 **WP:** pp. 21, 22, 23 **RW:** pp. 12, 13, 14 **SWT:** pp. B19, B20, B22, B23, B24, B25
Reading **HM Reading PE:** *2.2* pp. 398–399 **TE:** *2.2* pp. 151L, 153B–153E, 181N, 221N **PB:** *2.2* pp. 83, 108, 126, 211–212 **SWT:** pp. B19, B20, B22, B23, B24, B25

Personal Narrative *(continued)*

Score 1 **Benchmark Paper** The writer does not remain focused on the prompt. Instead of writing about the game received as a surprise, the writer lists many games. The narrative is short and disorganized. The paper also lacks a clear beginning, middle, and end. It has little elaboration and no supporting details. Word choice is limited (*us, game*). Sentences are simple and too similar in structure.

English **HM English** **PE:** pp. 67, 70–81 **TE:** pp. 71, 72, 74, 78 **WP:** pp. 21, 22, 23 **RW:** pp. 12, 13, 14
  SWT: pp. B4–B5, B14–B18, B19, B20, B23, B24, B25
Reading **HM Reading** **PE:** *2.2* pp. 398–399 **TE:** *2.1* p. 335N *2.2* pp. 152, 153A–153E, 181N, 221N **PB:** *2.1* p. 193
  2.2 pp. 108, 126, 211–212 **SWT:** pp. B4–B5, B14–B18, B19, B20, B23, B24, B25

Unscorable **Benchmark Paper** The paper is unscorable because the writer did not respond to the topic or type of writing specified in the prompt.

English **HM English** **PE:** p. 67 **SWT:** pp. B4–B5, B14–B18
Reading **HM Reading** **TE:** *2.2* p. 152 **SWT:** pp. B4–B5, B14–B18

Story   Score 4

Imagine that a child wakes up one morning with dark green skin and flippers for feet. This boy or girl has turned into a frog. What might happen after someone turns into a frog? Write a story for your classmates telling what happens.

"Ahhh! Mommy! Daddy!" Anna woke up and screamed for her parents when she saw that she had dark green, bumpy skin. Her parents didn't answer, so Anna jumped out of bed and went running to find them. She tripped and fell. Then she looked down and saw that she had flippers for feet! She didn't know what to do. Just then she heard a voice call, "Anna the frog, follow my voice."

Anna asked, "What happened? How did I become a frog?"

The voice called again, "Come, come, follow my voice." Anna took a step and suddenly fell into a deep dark tunnel. She kept falling and falling until she landed in a strange place filled with frogs!

"This is like a frog village or frog valley," said Anna.

Again she heard the voice call, "Follow me to the pool." Anna followed the voice and jumped into a beautiful clear blue pool. There were big green lily pads and beautiful flowers around the edge of the pool. Anna swam for hours with the other frogs. She was very tired when she finally left the pool.

more →

When Anna got out of the pool, the voice again said, "Anna, follow my voice. I've got something very special to show you." Anna followed the voice into a cave and saw a bed just like her own bed at home. Anna felt so tired that she lay down on the bed to rest. She had just fallen asleep when she heard a loud bang.

Anna opened her eyes and saw that the wind had blown her bedroom door shut. "Wait a minute," said Anna. "I was just in a cave. How did I get back to my bedroom?" Anna jumped out of bed and stared in the mirror. There were no flippers! Her skin wasn't green! She went running into her mom and dad's room to tell her parents all about her dream.

Story   Score 3

> Imagine that a child wakes up one morning with dark green skin and flippers for feet. This boy or girl has turned into a frog. What might happen after someone turns into a frog? Write a story for your classmates telling what happens.

One day as Max was waking up, he felt a little strange. He got out of bed and started hopping up and down. He saw that his skin was green and that his feet had turned into flippers. "Mom!" yelled Max. "I've turned into a frog!"

His mom called back, "Oh, stop being silly and come eat breakfast."

Max carefully hopped down the stairs. When he got into the kitchen, he saw a fly on his mom's nose. He quickly snatched up the fly with his long, slimy tongue. "Mmm, good breakfast," said Max. His mom fainted and fell to the floor.

Max got a glass of water and poured it on his mom's face. His mother opened her eyes.

"Mom, what do I do now?" asked Max.

Max tried to wash off the frog skin. It stayed green and bumpy. His mom tried to change his flippers into feet, but it didn't work. Max liked being a frog, so his mom took him to a pond and let him live there.

Story   Score 2

> Imagine that a child wakes up one morning with dark green skin and flippers for feet. This boy or girl has turned into a frog. What might happen after someone turns into a frog? Write a story for your classmates telling what happens.

Once a boy named Tim woke up. He had ugly, dark green hands and flippers. He stuck out his long tongue. He looked in the mirror. He had green skin. He jumped on the bed. Then he fell down.

Story **Score 1**

> Imagine that a child wakes up one morning with dark green skin and flippers for feet. This boy or girl has turned into a frog. What might happen after someone turns into a frog? Write a story for your classmates telling what happens.

A girl woke up, and she had ugly, dark green feet, and she went, "Croak!" She went to school. She didn't like being a frog. Frogs can jump. They can swim.

Story **Unscorable**

A frog has dark green skin. It has flippers for feet. Jump, jump, jump. A frog likes to jump. A frog sticks out its tongue to catch flies. Flies are very fast too. They buzz and buzz and tickle your face.

Story

Score 4   The paper is focused on the topic and purpose given in the prompt. An interesting problem grabs the reader's attention at the beginning, the middle is well developed, and the ending explains how the problem worked out. Rich details and exact words create clear pictures of characters, settings, and events. All events are important to the story. The story shows sentence variety and interesting language. Any mistakes do not distract.

Score 3   The paper is generally focused on the topic and purpose. The story has an obvious beginning, middle, and end, but they may be unevenly developed. Some events may be unimportant. More details and exact words would improve the story. Sentence variety and word choice can be improved. The few mistakes do not affect understanding.

Score 2   The paper may be vaguely focused on the topic and purpose. The story does not have a clear beginning, middle, or end. Many important events and details are missing or may not be clearly organized. Unimportant events or details detract from the story. Word choice is limited, and the paper lacks sentence variety. Some mistakes affect understanding.

Score 1   The paper is barely focused on the topic and purpose. The story is undeveloped and unorganized. The paper may be only a list of events. There is no identifiable beginning, middle, or end. There is little or no elaboration. There are few sentences, or they are short or unclear. Many mistakes affect understanding.

Unscorable   The paper doesn't respond to the prompt, may be illegible, or is written in a foreign language. The writer may do nothing more than restate the prompt, or the response may not be a story.

Story

Score 4 **Benchmark Paper** The writer has succeeded in telling a complete story that focuses on the topic in the prompt. The opening dialogue draws the reader into the story, and the events that follow are interesting, relevant, and told in a logical order. The ending clearly resolves the problem. The story includes ample supporting details (*bumpy skin, deep dark tunnel, beautiful clear blue pool*), and the continuous use of dialogue enhances the characters and events. The writing is lively, active, and clearly conveys the writer's strong voice. The main character, Anna, is authentic and plausible, and is developed through both dialogue and description. The sentences flow smoothly, and they vary in both type and structure.

Score 3 **Benchmark Paper** This is an appealing story that stays focused on the topic in the prompt. The paper is well-organized with a clear beginning, middle, and end. The events are told in a logical order, but the ending, in which Max moves to the pond, could use greater detail and elaboration. More support is needed to explain what Max liked about being a frog and how and why his mother decided to let him live in the pond. The writer uses precise vocabulary in many parts of the story (*snatched up the fly; long, slimy tongue; green and bumpy*). The sentences are varied and include some dialogue. They also flow well, making the story easy to read.

HM English **PE:** pp. 145, 146, 147, 148 **TE:** pp. 145, 146, 147 **WP:** pp. 50, 51, 52, 53, 54
  SWT: pp. B19, B20, B23, B24, B25
HM Reading **TE:** *2.1* pp. 41M–41N, 43A–43C, 43E **PB:** *2.1* pp. 18–19 **SWT:** pp. B19, B20, B23, B24, B25

Score 2 **Benchmark Paper** This writer deals with the topic minimally but does not focus effectively on the type of writing specified. As a story, the writing is undeveloped and poorly organized. The writer attempts to tell events in order, but the story has a short, uninteresting beginning sentence, and the problem is never resolved. Most of the narrative has very little supporting elaboration and detail. Word choice is imprecise. The piece is a short description rather than a real story. All sentences are short, simple, and lacking in variety.

HM English **PE:** pp. 145, 147, 148 **TE:** pp. 145, 147, 148 **WP:** pp. 50, 52, 53, 54 **RW:** pp. 31, 33, 34,
  35 **SWT:** pp. B19, B20, B22, B23, B24, B25
HM Reading **TE:** *2.1* pp. 43B–43E, 335N **PB:** *2.1* p. 193 **SWT:** pp. B19, B20, B22, B23, B24, B25

Story *(continued)*

Score 1 **Benchmark Paper** The writer restates parts of the prompt but fails to focus on the characteristics of a story. The writing is poorly organized; there is a beginning sentence but no middle or end. This writer needs more details and much more elaboration to develop a real plot and resolve the problem. The character is completely undeveloped, without even a name. Word choice is vague (*went, didn't like*). The first sentence is long and stringy and should be broken into shorter sentences. The remaining sentences are short, simple, and similar in structure.

HM English **PE:** pp. 139, 144–154 **TE:** pp. 144, 145, 146, 147, 152 **WP:** pp. 50, 51, 52, 53, 54 **RW:** pp. 31, 32, 33, 34, 35 **SWT:** pp. B6–B7, B14–B18, B19, B20, B23, B24

HM Reading **TE:** *2.1* pp. 42, 43A–43E **SWT:** pp. B6–B7, B14–B18, B19, B20, B23, B24

Unscorable **Benchmark Paper** The paper is unscorable because the writer did not respond to the type of writing specified in the prompt.

HM English **PE:** p. 139 **SWT:** pp. B6–B7, B14–B18

HM Reading **TE:** *2.1* p. 42 **SWT:** pp. B6–B7, B14–B18

Instructions   Score 4

> Think of one thing you know how to do well, such as riding a bike or making popcorn. Write instructions for your teacher telling how to do this activity. Be sure you explain all the steps.

Making a peanut butter and jelly sandwich is really easy. You will need two slices of fresh bread, a small plate, a jar of fruit jelly, a jar of creamy or crunchy peanut butter, and a table knife for spreading.

First, take one slice of bread and set it on the plate. Next, twist off the lid of the jar of peanut butter, carefully stick the knife in the jar, and lift out a small blob of peanut butter. Spread the peanut butter on one side of the slice of bread. Be sure to cover the whole slice, spreading the peanut butter to all four corners.

After wiping off the knife, open the jelly jar, slide out a small glob of jelly, and use the knife to spread the jelly on one side of the second slice of bread.

Last of all, squish the peanut butter and jelly sides of the bread together and your sandwich is done. Making a peanut butter and jelly sandwich is so much fun and so easy that you can do it all by yourself, but always remember to clean up and leave the kitchen as clean as you found it.

Instructions   **Score 3**

> Think of one thing you know how to do well, such as riding a
> bike or making popcorn. Write instructions for your teacher
> telling how to do this activity. Be sure you explain all the
> steps.

I will tell you how to clean out your desk. You will
need a trash can, paper towels, and some folders.
First, take all of the stuff out of your desk. Get rid
of any junk and old papers that you don't need and
put the papers that you want to keep in folders. Use
a paper towel to clean the inside of the desk. Stack
your folders and books neatly inside your desk. Finally,
put the rest of your stuff back in the desk. You can
quickly find what you are looking for when your desk
is clean.

Instructions   Score 2

> Think of one thing you know how to do well, such as riding a
> bike or making popcorn. Write instructions for your teacher
> telling how to do this activity. Be sure you explain all the
> steps.

Stand with your feet apart. Do cartwheels and land
on your feet. Start with your hands over your head.
Once I fell when I did a cartwheel. I hurt my knee.
Then I wore a brace on my knee when I did
gymnastics. You can do flips and jumps too.

Name _____

Instructions Score 1

> Think of one thing you know how to do well, such as riding a
> bike or making popcorn. Write instructions for your teacher
> telling how to do this activity. Be sure you explain all the
> steps.

My teddy bear goes on top. He goes on a pillow. I
have a blue bedspread. It is really warm and soft. I
pull up the covers.

Instructions Unscorable

I know how to do many things well. I know how to
do them well. I really know how.

Instructions

Score 4   The paper focuses on the topic and purpose given in the prompt. An interesting beginning sentence identifies the topic, and a strong ending wraps up the instructions. The writer tells all of the steps in order, using many order words, and includes all necessary materials. Many relevant details and exact words make each step clear. Sentences are written in different ways and flow smoothly. Any mistakes do not detract.

Score 3   The paper is generally focused on topic and purpose. The beginning identifies the topic but may be dull or flat. The ending may be uninteresting or incomplete. The steps are in order. More order words may be needed. The necessary materials are listed, but more specific details are needed to make some of the steps clear. Word choice and sentence variety can be improved. The few mistakes do not affect understanding.

Score 2   The paper is vaguely focused on topic and purpose. The beginning or ending may be weak or missing. Many steps may be sequenced incorrectly, and some steps may be missing. More order words are needed. Some materials may not be listed. Important details are missing or unclear. Word choice may be vague or awkward, and the paper lacks sentence variety. Some mistakes affect understanding.

Score 1   The paper is barely focused on topic and purpose. The instructions cannot be followed because the steps are not organized, are incomplete, and lack details. There are few sentences, or they are short or unclear. Many mistakes affect understanding.

Unscorable   The paper doesn't respond to the prompt, may be illegible, or is written in a foreign language. The writer may do nothing more than restate the prompt, or the response may not be a set of instructions.

Instructions

Score 4 **Benchmark Paper** The writer focuses on the topic and the prompt by writing clear and complete instructions telling how to make a peanut butter and jelly sandwich. The instructions are well organized, and all steps are presented in a logical order. The paper includes an effective topic sentence and an interesting ending sentence that wraps up the instructions. In this paper, the writer's word choice is exact and interesting *(twist off, blob, Spread, glob, squish)*. There are plenty of supporting details making each step clear enough so that the reader can easily follow the steps to make a sandwich. The writer uses order words *(First, Next, After, Last of all)* to tie the steps together. The paper contains sentences that are varied and that flow smoothly.

Score 3 **Benchmark Paper** The writer follows the prompt and writes on the topic of how to clean a desk. The steps are sequenced correctly, well written, and easy to follow. The writer includes a topic sentence and an interesting ending sentence. This paper includes the needed materials and all of the appropriate steps. There are no unnecessary ideas or details, but overall the paper needs more support and elaboration. Throughout, word choice is quite vague *(stuff, get rid of, junk)*. However, there is some variety in the structure of sentences, and the writer includes some order words to help the sentences flow smoothly.

English **HM English PE:** pp. 117, 185, 214, 220, H45 **WP:** pp. 49, 78, 79, 81, 82 **SWT:** pp. B19, B20, B23, B24, B25
Reading **HM Reading TE:** *2.1* p. 335N *2.2* pp. 327D–327E **PB:** *2.1* p. 193 *2.2* p. 173 **SWT:** pp. B19, B20, B23, B24, B25

Score 2 **Benchmark Paper** This essay is partly focused on the topic of how to do gymnastics, but the writer erroneously transitions to a personal narrative *(Once I fell . . . when I did gymnastics)*. In addition, the topic is too broad. The instructions should have been limited to one of the activities mentioned, such as the cartwheel. The paper does not include a topic sentence or an ending; it is poorly organized and confusing. Some steps are clearly out of order *(Start with your hands over your head.)*, and others are missing. The paper has few details. Each step needs to be better elaborated, and the writer fails to mention equipment needed. The relevant sentences are quite short and are not at all varied in structure. Order words would help the sentences to flow more smoothly.

English **HM English PE:** pp. 99–100, 171–172, 213–216, 220, H45 **WP:** pp. 31–32, 64–65, 79, 82 **RW:** pp. 19–20, 41–42, 50, 53 **SWT:** pp. B18, B19
Reading **HM Reading TE:** *2.2* pp. 181N, 221N, 325M–325N, 326, 327C–327E **PB:** *2.2* pp. 108, 126, 170, 173 **SWT:** pp. B18, B19

Instructions *(continued)*

Score 1 **Benchmark Paper** The writer has not stayed focused on the topic of making a bed; two of the five sentences contain only unrelated details. The few steps that are provided are out of order, and many others are missing. The writer does not include a topic sentence or an ending sentence. Much more support is needed to explain the steps, and imprecise words *(goes, covers)* contribute to the lack of clarity. There is no variety in the structure of the sentences.

English **HM English PE:** pp. 209, 212–216 **WP:** pp. 79–82 **RW:** pp. 50–52 **SWT:** pp. B18, B19

Reading **HM Reading TE:** *2.2* pp. 181N, 325M–325N, 326, 327A–327E **PB:** *2.2* pp. 108, 170, 173
SWT: pp. B18, B19

Unscorable **Benchmark Paper** This paper is unscorable because the response is simply a rewording of the prompt.

English **HM English SWT:** pp. B8–B9, B16–B18 **Reading** **HM Reading SWT:** pp. B8–B9, B16–B18

Name _____

Description   Score 4

> Choose a pet that you like very much. It could be your own pet or a pet that belongs to someone else. Write a description of this pet for your teacher. Use as many senses as you can. Be sure to include lots of details.

I have a beautiful pet hamster who is my best friend. I call him Snuggles because his tan and white fur is really soft and cuddly. His eyes are as red as a fire engine.

Snuggles has a nose that is icy cold, like a snowball. It's soaking wet too! Snuggles squeals when I hold him. When he squeals, it sounds like he is singing. Sometimes he smells really stinky, like garbage left in the hot sun. Most of the time Snuggles smells very fresh. Snuggles likes to wash himself with his pink tongue. That way he stays clean. I help him by cleaning his cage every few days. I love taking care of Snuggles, and he loves me!

Name _____

Description   Score 3

Choose a pet that you like very much. It could be your own pet or a pet that belongs to someone else. Write a description of this pet for your teacher. Use as many senses as you can. Be sure to include lots of details.

My cat is about seven years old. She is called Mia because of the sound she makes. She is kind of big. She is as black as a black crayon and has white whiskers. She has green eyes. She has a flat, brown nose. Her fur is really nice. Most of the day she naps. She has long claws. She scratches things with her claws. Once she even scratched our sofa. When she naps, she curls up on the sofa. She purrs really loudly when she napping. She likes to play with things. She is a good cat.

Name _____

Description   Score 2

Choose a pet that you like very much. It could be your own pet or a pet that belongs to someone else. Write a description of this pet for your teacher. Use as many senses as you can. Be sure to include lots of details.

Carrots has long ears. I named her Carrots. She does lots of things. I'm happy I got Carrots. I almost got a dog, but then I got Carrots. We can't have a dog too. My best friend got a dog. Sometimes Carrots makes noises. I always play with her. She has a cage. She is brown except her tail is white. Some rabbits are all white. They have red eyes.

Name _____

Description `Score 1`

> Choose a pet that you like very much. It could be your own pet or a pet that belongs to someone else. Write a description of this pet for your teacher. Use as many senses as you can. Be sure to include lots of details.

Turtles have shells. They live in the water. I like turtles.

Description `Unscorable`

I don't like any pets. The End.

Description

___

Score 4   The writing is clearly focused on the topic and the purpose given in the prompt. The topic is introduced in an interesting way. The details are well organized and presented in an order that makes sense. The writer draws on a variety of senses and describes the topic using many interesting sensory details and exact, colorful words that create a vivid mental picture. Sentences are varied and flow smoothly. Any mistakes do not detract.

___

Score 3   The writing is focused on the topic and purpose. The paper describes the topic clearly. Most details are presented in a logical order, although one or two details may be out of place. More elaboration would improve the paper, and word choice may not always be exact. The paper may lack sentence variety. The few mistakes do not affect understanding.

___

Score 2   The writing may be vaguely focused on the topic and purpose. The beginning does not clearly state the topic or may be missing. Many details are missing or unrelated; the details that are included are disorganized. Word choice is limited, and the paper lacks sentence variety. Some mistakes affect understanding.

___

Score 1   The writing is barely focused on the topic and purpose. The paper may lack any sense of organization. There is no elaboration with sensory details. There are few sentences, or they are short or unclear. Many mistakes affect understanding.

___

Unscorable   The response doesn't answer the prompt at all. It may be illegible or written in a foreign language. It may do nothing more than restate the prompt, or it may be a copy of a published work.

Description

Score 4 **Benchmark Paper** The writing is tightly focused on the topic and purpose given in the prompt. The paper is well organized. The topic is introduced in a clear and interesting way and conveys the writer's enthusiasm, and the details are presented in a logical order. Colorful sensory details and exact word choice help readers see (*tan and white fur*), hear (*squeals*), feel (*soft and cuddly, icy cold*), and smell (*stinky, fresh*) the hamster. Similes (*as red as a fire engine, like a snowball*) add clarity and freshness to the description. Sentence fluency is strong. The writer has varied the structure of sentences; short sentences are often combined (*I call him Snuggles because his tan and white fur is really soft and cuddly.*)

Score 3 **Benchmark Paper** The writing is focused on the topic and purpose. The paper is generally well organized and states the topic. Although most details are in a logical order, the details about the cat napping are not all grouped together. The writer uses some sensory details and exact words (*white whiskers; green eyes; flat, brown nose; long claws*) and includes a simile (*as black as a black crayon*). However, more elaboration is needed (additional details about the cat's fur and what the cat likes to play with) to make the description more vivid. Word choice is often vague (*kind of big, nice, things*). Some sentences are varied, but many are short and begin the same way (*She*).

English **HM English PE:** pp. 245–246, 251–252, 275–276, 282   **WP:** pp. 89, 90, 95, 96, 98, 101–102
   SWT: pp. B19, B21, B25, B29

Reading **HM Reading TE:** *2.1* pp. 155C–155E, 209N, 335N *2.2* p. 221N   **PB:** *2.1* pp. 124, 193 *2.2* p. 126
   SWT: pp. B19, B21, B25, B29

Score 2 **Benchmark Paper** The writing is vaguely focused on the topic and purpose. The paper has little sense of organization. The description begins abruptly and does not clearly state the topic. There are few sensory details. A number of details do not keep to the topic, and the order of details is random and confusing. Word choice is limited, making the rabbit hard to picture. Sentences are short and almost unvaried in structure.

English **HM English PE:** pp. 99–100, 171–172, 274–276, 278, 282   **WP:** pp. 31–32, 64–65, 98, 100, 101, 102
   RW: pp. 19, 20, 41, 42, 64, 66, 67, 68   **SWT:** pp. B19, B20, B30

Reading **HM Reading TE:** *2.1* pp. 155A–155E, 177N *2.2* p. 181N   **PB:** *2.1* p. 107 *2.2* p. 108   **SWT:** pp. B19, B20, B30

Description (continued)

Score 1 **Benchmark Paper** The writing barely addresses the topic and purpose. The beginning does not clearly state the topic, and there is no elaboration with sensory words and details. The writer does not draw on any senses. There are few sentences, and word choice is limited. The sentences are short and unvaried.

HM English PE: pp. 271, 274–276 **WB:** pp. 98, 101 **RW:** pp. 64, 67 **SWT:** pp. B19, B20
HM Reading TE: *2.1* pp. 154, 155A–155E, 177N *2.2* p. 181N **PB:** *2.1* p. 107 *2.2* p. 108
SWT: pp. B19, B20

Unscorable **Benchmark Paper** This paper is unscorable because the writer does not respond to the topic and the purpose in the prompt.

HM English SWT: pp. B8, B9, B16, B17 **HM Reading SWT:** pp. B8, B9, B16, B17

Name _____

Opinion Essay/Explanation   Score 4

> Many people enjoy taking car trips. Write a paper for your teacher telling why it is fun to take car trips.

Every year my family takes a long car trip to my grandma's house in New Mexico. It takes three full days to get there, so I really know many of the wonderful things about car trips.

I really enjoy taking car trips because there are so many different things to do. My mom always brings interesting items to keep me busy. She usually packs puzzles, books, games, and videos. Watching funny movies and cartoons on the tiny television really makes the time fly by. I also enjoy playing games with my sister. We like to play Concentration, Go Fish, and checkers. I also read books and do crossword puzzles when my sister and I are tired of playing games.

Another thing that I love about taking car trips is sleeping in the car. During the day when I'm tired, I just plop my head down on my big, soft pillow to sleep. Each night when I'm really exhausted, I crawl into my cozy sleeping bag in the back of the car.

I think road trips are absolutely terrific!

Name _____

Opinion Essay/Explanation Score 3

Many people enjoy taking car trips. Write a paper for your teacher telling why it is fun to take car trips.

There are many things that I like about car trips. I enjoy trips by car because I can do interesting activities by myself such as playing games and listening to the radio. My family and I also visit lots of exciting places. Another good thing about car trips is that I get to spend time with my family. We talk about school and my soccer team. We also do a lot of cool things together. I like playing word games and singing songs with my mom, dad, and brother. I really enjoy trips in the car and spending the time with my family.

Name _____

Opinion Essay/Explanation

Many people enjoy taking car trips. Write a paper for your teacher telling why it is fun to take car trips.

Car trips are good because you get to stop if you want to. I like going out to eat. I like staying in hotels. It is fun. I also like being with my family. I like visiting my cousins.

Name _____

Opinion Essay/Explanation   `Score 1`

> Many people enjoy taking car trips. Write a paper for your teacher telling why it is fun to take car trips.

My dad has a big new car. We went on a long car trip. I played a game. It was fun! Then I was tired.

Opinion Essay/Explanation   `Unscorable`

Once there was a boy named Marco. He went on a long car trip from Jacksonville to Miami. He said, "This is fun!"

Opinion Essay/Explanation

Score 4 The paper is focused on the topic and purpose given in the prompt. The essay is well organized. The opening states the writer's feeling clearly, and the closing sums them up. The reasons are strong, and specific examples support each reason. All of the details go with the reasons they support. Word choice is exact and interesting, and the voice conveys the writer's feelings. Sentences are varied and flow smoothly. Any mistakes do not detract.

Score 3 The paper is focused on the topic and purpose. The opening may be uninteresting, or the closing may not effectively sum up the writer's ideas. The writer gives good reasons, but one or more reasons may need more support or may be not be totally relevant. Word choice may be inexact and may not effectively convey the writer's feelings. Sentence variety could be improved. The few mistakes do not affect understanding.

Score 2 The paper is vaguely focused on the topic and purpose. The opening or closing may be missing. Supporting reasons and examples may be irrelevant or inadequate. Ideas and details may not be well organized. Word choice may be inexact, and the writer's voice may be weak. The paper lacks sentence variety. Some mistakes affect understanding.

Score 1 The paper is barely focused on the topic and purpose. The essay is not developed with reasons and details that support an opinion. There are few sentences, or they are short or unclear. Many mistakes affect understanding.

Unscorable The paper doesn't respond to the prompt, is illegible, or is written in a foreign language. The writer may do nothing more than restate the prompt, or the response may not be an expository essay that explains why.

Opinion Essay/Explanation

Score 4 **Benchmark Paper** The writing remains focused on the topic as the writer explains why he or she thinks car trips are enjoyable. The essay begins with an opening that clearly states the writer's feelings. The writer has also included two strong supporting reasons and has provided good examples to back up each reason. The closing sums up the writer's feelings in an interesting way. Word choice is exact and helps to demonstrate the writer's strong feelings (*wonderful, funny movies and cartoons, plop my head down, crawl, cozy sleeping bag*). Connecting devices (*also, Another*) are used to tie the sentences together and to help the writing flow smoothly. The writer has also varied the structure and the beginnings of sentences throughout the paper.

Score 3 **Benchmark Paper** The writing is focused on the topic, and the writer's feelings are explained clearly and in a way that makes sense. The writer includes several strong reasons along with examples supporting some of the reasons. The closing, however, is weak and does not effectively sum up the writer's thoughts and feelings. More details are also needed to describe the games that are played, what the writer listens to on the radio, and the places that are visited. Word choice is often inexact (*good thing, cool things*) and does not effectively convey the writer's voice. Some sentences are varied, but additional transitional words are needed to help the sentences flow more smoothly.

English **HM English** **PE:** pp. 349, 350, 351, 352, 356 **WP:** pp. 125, 126, 127, 128, 129 **SWT:** pp. B19, B23, B24, B25
Reading **HM Reading** **TE:** *2.1* p. 335N *2.2* pp. 151M–151N **PB:** *2.1* p. 193 *2.2* pp. 84–85 **SWT:** pp. B19, B23, B24, B25

Score 2 **Benchmark Paper** The paper is somewhat focused on the topic. The opening expresses the writer's feelings, but there is no closing. The writer has included two reasons to like car trips. However, the first reason and its supporting examples (*going out to eat, staying in hotels*) are not totally relevant, and no examples support the second reason. Much more elaboration is needed throughout. The writer has used inexact words (*good, like, fun*) that contribute to a lack of voice. The sentences are very similar in structure; most begin in the same way.

English **HM English** **PE:** pp. 78, 349, 350, 351, 352, 356 **TE:** pp. 78, 350, 351, 352, 356 **WP:** pp. 24, 125, 126, 127, 128, 129 **RW:** pp. 15, 81, 82, 83, 84, 85 **SWT:** pp. B19, B20, B21, B23, B24, B25, B29, B30
Reading **HM Reading** **TE:** *2.1* pp. 177M–177N, 335N, 367N *2.2* pp. 151M–151N, 181N, 221N **PB:** *2.1* pp. 106–107, 193, 211 *2.2* pp. 84–85, 108, 126 **SWT:** pp. B19, B20, B21, B23, B24, B25, B29, B30

Opinion Essay/Explanation *(continued)*

Score 1 **Benchmark Paper** This paper is barely focused on the topic. The composition does not have an opening or a closing, and there are no clear reasons or examples explaining why the writer enjoys car trips. The essay includes two extraneous details (*My dad has a big new car. . . . Then I was tired.*), and much more elaboration and additional supporting details are needed throughout. All of the sentences are short and structurally similar, and they do not flow smoothly.

English **HM English** **PE:** pp. 345, 348–358 **TE:** pp. 350, 351, 352, 356 **WP:** pp. 125, 126, 127, 128, 129 **RW:** pp. 81, 82, 83, 84, 85 **SWT:** pp. B10–B11, B14–B18, B19, B20, B21, B22
Reading **HM Reading** **TE:** *2.1* pp. 177M–177N, 367N *2.2* pp. 151M–151N, 181N, 221N **PB:** *2.1* pp. 106–107, 211 *2.2* pp. 84–85, 108, 126 **SWT:** pp. B9–B10, B14–B18, B19, B20, B21, B22

Unscorable **Benchmark Paper** This writing is unscorable because it is a narrative rather than an expository paper, and it does not adequately respond to the topic in the prompt.

English **HM English** **PE:** p. 345 **SWT:** pp. B10–B11, B14–B18 **Reading** **HM Reading** **SWT:** pp. B9–B10, B14–B18

Name _____

Persuasive Essay `Score 4`

> Which animal do you think would make the best pet for your classroom? Write an essay for your teacher. Tell what kind of pet you think your class should have. Give reasons for your answer.

Having a classroom pet is a wonderful idea! There are many different types of animals that would make a good pet, but I think that a rabbit would make a perfect classroom pet.

A rabbit is a terrific pet for a classroom for a couple of reasons. First, since rabbits are very quiet animals, a rabbit in the classroom would not bother us when we are working. A rabbit makes sounds only when it is quietly munching on lettuce and carrots or hopping softly around its cage. Other pets, like gerbils, make a lot of noise scratching, digging, and running on their exercise wheels. Having a rabbit in the classroom would not distract us.

Second, rabbits are very friendly and gentle animals. They enjoy being held and petted. A pet rabbit would not bite or hurt the children in our classroom.

If our class is going to get a pet, don't you think that a quiet, cuddly, and gentle animal is best? A rabbit would definitely make a super classroom pet! Our class should have one to love and care for.

Persuasive Essay   Score 3

Which animal do you think would make the best pet for your classroom? Write an essay for your teacher. Tell what kind of pet you think your class should have. Give reasons for your answer.

I think we should have a turtle for a classroom pet. A turtle is very easy to take care of, and it is also interesting to watch. Caring for a turtle is very easy and takes very little time. All you have to do is give it some food and water every day and clean its tank once or twice a week. I feed my dog every day. It's easy. The children in our class can take turns caring for the turtle. Watching a turtle is also very interesting. I like to watch it move. Sometimes the turtle doesn't move. I think we should get a turtle because it is easy to care for and fun to look at.

Name _____

Persuasive Essay   Score 2

Which animal do you think would make the best pet for your classroom? Write an essay for your teacher. Tell what kind of pet you think your class should have. Give reasons for your answer.

I want you to get a goldfish as a pet for our classroom. It is fun to watch a goldfish swim in a big bowl. A goldfish is a good pet for schools. It won't keep us from doing our work.

Name _____

Persuasive Essay   **Score 1**

> Which animal do you think would make the best pet for your classroom? Write an essay for your teacher. Tell what kind of pet you think your class should have. Give reasons for your answer.

We could have many different kinds of pets in our classroom. We could have cats, dogs, fish, birds, lizards, snakes, and turtles. They would make great pets.

Persuasive Essay   **Unscorable**

I like gerbils. I think gerbils are fun. I have a gerbil at home. He is cute. Kittens are cute too. My gerbil's name is Fluffy.

Persuasive Essay

Score 4   The writing is focused on the topic, purpose, and audience given in the prompt. The essay is well organized. The opening states the goal clearly, the middle explains the reasons, and the closing sums up the reasons. The reasons are strong and are supported with facts or examples. All of the details go with the reasons they support. Word choice is exact and interesting, and the voice conveys the writer's feelings. Sentence structure is varied and smooth. Any mistakes do not detract.

Score 3   The writing is generally focused on the topic, purpose, and audience, but some irrelevant ideas may be included. The opening or closing may be weak. The writer gives good reasons, but one or more reasons may need more support to be clear or convincing. All of the details go with the reasons they support. The writer's voice may be weak. Word choice and sentence variety can be improved. The few mistakes do not affect understanding.

Score 2   The writing may be vaguely focused on the topic, purpose, and audience. The opening or closing may be missing, and some details may be misplaced. The writer might not have included enough reasons, and the reasons are inadequately supported. Some of the support may be irrelevant. Word choice may be limited, and the voice is generally weak. The paper lacks sentence variety. Some mistakes affect understanding.

Score 1   The writing is barely focused on the topic, purpose, and audience. There is no clear goal or reasons. There are no supporting facts or examples, or the support may be irrelevant. There are few sentences, or they are short or unclear. Many mistakes affect understanding.

Unscorable   The response doesn't answer the prompt at all. It may be illegible or written in a foreign language. It may merely restate the prompt, or it may not be a persuasive essay.

Persuasive Essay

Score 4 **Benchmark Paper** The writing is focused on the topic, purpose, and audience given in the prompt. The paper is well organized with an interesting opening that clearly states the goal, a middle that explains the reasons, and a closing that sums up the reasons. The writer gives two strong reasons in separate paragraphs and supports each one with ample facts and examples. Connecting words (*First, Second*) make clear transitions between the reasons. Exact and vivid word choice (*bother, quietly munching, hopping softly, scratching, distract, friendly and gentle*) help to create this paper's strong voice. The writer has varied sentence beginnings, structure, and length.

Score 3 **Benchmark Paper** The writing generally stays focused on the topic, purpose, and audience. The paper is well organized. It begins with a clear statement of the writer's goal. The writer continues by including two reasons and ends with a good closing sentence. The first reason is sufficiently elaborated, but the second reason needs more support. (What else does a turtle do that is interesting?) The writer has included extraneous details with each reason (*I feed my dog…It's easy; Sometimes the turtle doesn't move.*). More exact words and details are needed to make the writing clearer and more interesting to read and to give it some voice. The writer varies the beginnings and structure of sentences but overuses several words (*very easy, caring for, watch, interesting*).

HM English PE: pp. 117, 185, 245–246, 350, 352, 366 **WP:** pp. 49, 78, 89–90, 125, 127, 128 **SWT:** pp. B19, B24, B26

HM Reading TE: *2.1* pp. 209N, 335N, 367M–367N *2.2* pp. 151N, 181N, 327E **PB:** *2.1* pp. 124, 193, 210–211 *2.2* pp. 85, 108, 173 **SWT:** pp. B19, B24, B26

Score 2 **Benchmark Paper** The writer remains focused on the topic, purpose, and audience. This essay opens with a sentence stating a goal, but the closing is missing. The writer provides two reasons (*It is fun to watch…; A goldfish is a good pet for schools.*), but there are no facts or examples to support the reasons for wanting a goldfish as a pet. Much more elaboration is needed, and word choice is limited. The sentences are short, but the writer has varied their beginnings.

HM English PE: pp. 99, 117, 171, 185, 350, 351, 356, 366–367 **WP:** pp. 31–32, 49, 65, 78, 125, 126 **RW:** pp. 20, 30, 41, 49, 81, 82 **SWT:** pp. B19, B25, B30

HM Reading TE: *2.1* pp. 263N, 367M–367N *2.2* pp. 181N, 221N, 327E **PB:** *2.1* pp. 152, 210–211 *2.2* pp. 108, 126, 173 **SWT:** pp. B19, B25, B30

Persuasive Essay (continued)

Score 1 **Benchmark Paper** The writing barely addresses the topic, purpose, and audience. The paper is little more than a list of different types of pets. There is no clear goal, and the paper is lacking in reasons, facts, and examples. Word choice is uninteresting, and voice is missing.

English **HM English PE:** pp. 362–367 **TE:** pp. 362–367 **SWT:** pp. B19, B20
Reading **HM Reading TE:** *2.1* pp. 177M–177N, 367M–367N **PB:** *2.1* pp. 106–107, 210–211 **SWT:** pp. B19, B20

Unscorable **Benchmark Paper** This paper is unscorable because it does not respond to the prompt. The writer is simply stating an opinion and does not attempt to persuade.

English **HM English SWT:** pp. B12, B13, B16–B18 Reading **HM Reading SWT:** pp. B12, B13, B16–B18

Practice Tests: Answer Key

Belling the Cat (pp. A18–A19)

1. *Sample high-scoring response:* It is a problem that the cat is very quiet. The cat can sneak up on the mice before they know it. (Understanding Stories)

2. *Sample high-scoring response:* The little mouse's plan might not work because no one will want to hang the bell on the cat's neck. The mouse who tries to do it might get caught and hurt by the cat. (Main Idea and Supporting Details)

Meet Beatrix Potter (pp. A20–A21)

1. *Sample high-scoring response:* Beatrix Potter wanted her books to be small. She wanted them to fit in a child's hands. (Main Idea and Supporting Details)

2. *Sample high-scoring response:* Beatrix Potter liked to write books about animals. She wrote about rabbits and squirrels and other animals. She also liked to write about the country. (Main Idea and Supporting Details)

How a Mosquito Grows Up (pp. A22–A23)

1. *Sample high-scoring response:* The larva sticks the tube out of the water. Then the larva breathes in air from above the water. (Words and Pictures)

2. *Sample high-scoring response:* You would find more mosquitoes in a swamp. This is because most mosquito eggs hatch in water. Then mosquitoes live in the water until they grow their wings. (Main Idea and Supporting Details)

Elaboration Strategies Answer Key

Using Exact Details (p. B19)
1. Mia built a huge castle with towers.
2. We found shells and crabs.
3. It was the best day of the summer!
4. *Sample:* We ate pizza and ice cream at the beach.

Asking and Answering Questions (p. B20)
1. A spotted toad hopped on the rock.
2. My mom sang with my dad for a music show.
3. *Sample:* One red balloon floated into the air.
4. *Sample:* Yesterday a freight train stopped slowly at the station.
5. *Sample:* The huge dog barked loudly from the porch.

Using Sensory Words (p. B21)
Samples:
1. The soft hay smelled sweet.
2. A loud tractor scared the tiny bunnies.
3. Sue and I picked fresh, juicy berries.
4. At the cookout, long metal tables were set up near the tall wooden fence.
5. We had fresh bread, yellow corn, and juicy watermelon for lunch.

Using *on, at, in,* and *with* to Add Details (p. B22)
1. Meg hit the ball with her bat.
2. Ben stepped on first base.
3. He caught the ball in his glove.
4–6. *Sample:*
   Our family went to a funny restaurant with our neighbors. We had a big table in the basement. There were silly pictures on the floor.

Using Exact Nouns (p. B23)
1. teacher
2. books
3. computer
4. oceans

5–10. *Sample:*
   Once upon a time, there was a prince who lived in a big castle. One day he went for a walk with his tiger. They walked to a forest and saw a big bush near a tree. He wondered if birds lived there.

Using Exact Verbs (p. B24)
1. whispered
2. spotted
3. dashed
4. hid

5–10. *Sample:*
   I love my new computer game! A spaceship races across the screen. Space rocks zoom toward you. The captain shouts if a rock gets too close. The rocks explode if you hit them. The goal is to land on all of the planets.

Using Exact Adjectives (p. B25)
1. huge
2. tiny
3. colorful
4. brief
5. *Sample:* Our family took a great trip.
6. *Sample:* We went on some exciting rides.
7. *Sample:* The speedy roller coaster was my favorite.
8. *Sample:* I had a frozen drink at the park.

Using Adverbs (p. B26)
Samples:
1. proudly
2. slowly
3. gently
4. quietly
5. We ran excitedly to the ticket booth.
6. Mom cheerfully asked for six circus tickets.
7. The lion tamer moved carefully.
8. The seals barked loudly.

Using Similes (p. B27)

1. The alarm sounded like a howling wolf.
2. My feet felt as icy as an igloo.
3. The baby's eyes were like twinkling stars.
4. *Sample:* The clouds looked like dancing sheep.
5. *Sample:* Our classroom was as quiet as a sleeping baby.
6. *Sample:* The man's voice sounds like a barking seal.

Using Sound Words (p. B28)

1. clang
2. crash
3. peep
4. hiss
5. pop
6. *Sample:* The little kitten meowed to ask for milk.
7. *Sample:* The thunder boomed in the mountains.
8. *Sample:* The bee buzzed as it landed on the flower.

Beginning Sentences in Different Ways (p. B29)

Samples:
1. They played on the swings.
2. All of the kids zoomed down the slide.
3. The boys and girls had lots of fun.
4–5. *Sample:*
    My teacher took us to a science museum. She showed us some dinosaurs. Juan and I saw dinosaur eggs. We touched a dinosaur bone.

Using Different Kinds of Sentences (p. B30)

Samples:
1. Are the animals fun to watch?
2. Go to the zoo tomorrow.
3. You will have a great time!

4–6. *Sample:*
Grandma gave me a puppy. I am teaching him tricks. Sparky can do a lot already. He can roll over and sit. He can even catch a ball! Do you think he is a smart puppy? Come over to meet him soon.